12.95
SSA

★ ★ ★ ★ ★

PRESIDENT'S COMMISSION
FOR A NATIONAL AGENDA FOR THE EIGHTIES

REPORT OF THE PANEL ON
POLICIES AND PROSPECTS FOR
METROPOLITAN AND NONMETROPOLITAN AMERICA

Urban America
IN THE
Eighties
PERSPECTIVES
AND PROSPECTS

PRENTICE-HALL, INC., Englewood Cliffs, New Jersey 07632

A SPECTRUM BOOK

This document was prepared by the Panel on Policies and Prospects for Metropolitan and Nonmetropolitan America in the Eighties, one of nine Panels of the President's Commission for a   National Agenda for the Eighties. The report represents the views of a majority of members of the Panel on each point considered. Not every member of the Panel agrees with or supports every view or recommendation in the report. This report was prepared by members of the Panel without involvement by members of the Commission who were not members of the Panel. This project was supported by the U.S. Department of Housing and Urban Development, under provisions of Executive Order No. 12168, October 24, 1979. Points of view or opinions expressed in this volume are those of the Panel on Policies and Prospects for Metropolitan and Nonmetropolitan America in the Eighties, and do not necessarily represent the official position of the U.S. Department of Housing and Urban Development.

Library of Congress Cataloging in Publication Data

United States. Panel on Policies and Prospects for
    Metropolitan and Nonmetropolitan America.
    Urban America in the eighties.

    (A Spectrum book)
    At head of title: President's Commission for a
National Agenda for the Eighties.
    Reprint. Originally published: Washington: President's
Commission for a National Agenda for the Eighties, 1980.
    Includes index.
    1. Urban policy—United States—Congresses.
I. United States. President's Commission for a
National Agenda for the Eighties. II. Title.
HT123.U466   1981   307.7′6′0973   81-8831
                                        AACR2
ISBN 0-13-939603-9
ISBN 0-13-939553-9 {PBK}

Foreword

As America enters the eighties, our nation faces a world greatly changed from that of even a decade ago. Vast forces are in action at home and abroad that promise to change the lives of all Americans. Some of these forces—such as revolutionary developments in science and technology—hold out hope for longer life, labor-saving mechanisms, exploration of the universe, and other benefits for all peoples. Other forces—such as the growing demand for strategic raw materials under the control of supplier cartels—raise serious problems for all nations. At home, we face serious and unresolved issues in the social and economic structure of American society.

On October 24, 1979, President Jimmy Carter established the President's Commission for a National Agenda for the Eighties. His purpose was to provide the President-elect and the new Congress with the views of 45 Americans drawn from diverse backgrounds outside of government. The group is bipartisan, representing business and labor, science and the humanities, arts and communication. Members of the Commission are experts in many fields, but possess no special expertise in predicting the future. Rather, we have done our best to uncover the dynamics of American society and world affairs that we believe will determine events in the eighties. This report of the Commission, *A National Agenda for the Eighties,* sets forth our views.

The analytical work of the Commission was accomplished by 9 Panels, each consisting of 5 to 11 Commissioners with appropriate staff. The Panels probed into major subject areas designated by the President in the Executive Order that created the Commission, as well as other areas that the Commission itself determined should be on the agenda. This approach gave Panel members an opportunity to gain considerable familiarity with complex subject matters, and provided the full Commission with a wide range of information not otherwise attainable in the 13 months available for this study.

The Panels are responsible for their own reports, and the views contained in any Panel report do not necessarily reflect the views of any branch of government or of the Commission as a whole.

William J. McGill/Chairman
La Jolla, California/December 31, 1980

PRESIDENT'S COMMISSION
FOR A NATIONAL

Agenda
FOR THE
Eighties

Chairman
William J. McGill

Daniel Bell	Ruth J. Hinerfeld	Frank Pace, Jr.
Robert S. Benson	Carl Holman	Edmund D. Pellegrino
Charles E. Bishop	Benjamin L. Hooks	Donald C. Platten
Gwendolyn Brooks	Matina S. Horner	Tomás Rivera
J. Fred Bucy, Jr.	Thomas C. Jorling	Paul G. Rogers
Pastora San Juan Cafferty	Rhoda H. Karpatkin	Elspeth D. Rostow
Joan Ganz Cooney	Lane Kirkland	Howard J. Samuels
Marian Wright Edelman	Juanita M. Kreps	Henry B. Schacht
Herman E. Gallegos	Esther Landa	William W. Scranton
John W. Gardner	Theodore R. Marmor	Lewis Thomas
Don L. Gevirtz	Martin E. Marty	Foy Valentine
C. Jackson Grayson, Jr.	Michael McCloskey	Glenn E. Watts
Philip Handler	William E. Miller	Marina v. N. Whitman
Dorothy I. Height	Alan B. Morrison	Addie L. Wyatt
William A. Hewitt	Roger G. Noll	

Co-Staff Directors
Claude E. Barfield   Richard A. Wegman

Preface

The United States has become a predominantly urban nation during this century. However, only very gradually have we come to understand that this description indicates less about where people live than about the circumstances that define peoples' lives. During the second half of the 20th century, our nation commenced vigorous efforts to understand and respond to changes in and around our nation's settlements—changes that were already well advanced during the first half of the century. Such are the lags that occur between our experiencing change and our recognizing and responding to it.

Changing conditions and circumstances that Americans have come to define as "urban problems." like the policies and programs proposed through the years to deal with them, are all derivative from basic forces operating in our society and the world. The metaphors that we employ to describe these conditions (city "decline," "death," or "urban sprawl") do much to influence how and whether urban policy issues are debated. It was against this background that the Panel on Policies and Prospects for Metropolitan and Nonmetropolitan America in the Eighties undertook the preparation of this report.

Our Panel included Mr. Robert S. Benson, President of Children's World, Inc.; Professor Pastora San Juan Cafferty, School of Social Service Administration, University of Chicago; Ms. Ruth J. Hinerfeld, President of the League of Women Voters; and Mr. Frank Pace, Jr., President and Chief Executive Officer of the International Executive Service Corps. As Panel Chair, I welcomed the diversity of talents, interests, and backgrounds brought by the Panel members to the task.

Our goal has been to prepare a document that views the changes shaping urban America in the broadest possible context. We have attempted to prepare a report that will stimulate debate, encourage the reconceptualization of problems, distinguish long-term policy strategies from short-term transitional initiatives, and sketch the broader outlines of an appropriate federal urban policy role for the decade ahead. In order to focus attention sharply on the major dynamic forces shaping urban America, we have restricted our comments to issues of urban growth and development. Such policy areas as housing, transportation, poverty, employment, or environmental protection, while all highly important topics worthy of careful study, have of necessity been secondary to our more central focus.

With limited time and resources available, we thought it best to attempt to examine the background forces that provide the context within which substantive policy issues must be defined and debated. Further, we have not sought to delineate a separate rural agenda since one of our major premises is that the distinctions between urban and rural—as well as intrametropolitan and interregional—are being blurred by processes of social and economic transformation taking place across our nation.

Throughout the past year, our Panel placed a greater premium on probing traditional assumptions and confronting conventional wisdom than on striving for consensus and unanimity. Accordingly, not all the recommendations and interpretations across the several issue areas are supported by all of the Panel members. But again, our purpose is to stimulate discussion and debate, not foreclose it.

Throughout the year, we benefitted from the cooperation of and contributions from sources too numerous to list here. The Panel solicited and received information and opinion from a wide variety of local, county, state, and federal governmental officials, academics, researchers, interest groups and professional organization membership, and public hearings throughout the nation. We established a State and Local Advisory Board composed of representatives of the National Association of Counties, the National Conference of State Legislatures, the National Governors' Association, the Council of State Governments, the International City Management Association, the National League of Cities, and the United States Conference of Mayors. During the year, we circulated drafts and scheduled meetings in order to have the benefit of their counsel on difficult issues.

The Panel wishes to extend its special appreciation to the Assembly of Behavioral and Social Sciences of the National Academy of Sciences for cosponsoring a 2-day symposium at which the Panel and staff sought and received the counsel of many of the nation's foremost students of urban problems and policies. Additionally, the Panel wishes to express its gratitude to numerous fellow Commissioners who, although not members of this Panel, contributed to its deliberations throughout the year. To the several scholars and researchers who were commissioned to prepare background papers or who contributed papers for our consideration, we also owe a debt of gratitude. The able direction of Claude E. Barfield and Richard A. Wegman, Staff Directors, and the helpful insights of Raymond F. Reisler, Senior Professional Staff, and the efforts of Lewis D. Gitlin, Research Assistant, and Judith Ross Ferguson, editor, as well as those contributions from other Panel staff members and the administrative support staff, are gratefully acknowledged. Finally, we wish to extend our sincere appreciation to Donald A. Hicks, Senior Professional Staff, who wrote the Panel report and who together with Diane Knight, Professional Staff, was responsible for the day-to-day conduct of the Panel's activities.

Charles E. Bishop

Charles E. Bishop
Panel Chairperson

Houston, Texas
December 31, 1980

Metropolitan America

POLICIES AND PROSPECTS FOR

AND NONMETROPOLITAN

Chairperson
Charles E. Bishop
President
University of Houston System

Robert S. Benson
President, Children's
World, Inc.

Ruth J. Hinerfeld
President, League of
Women Voters

Pastora San Juan Cafferty
Professor, School of Social
Service Administration,
University of Chicago

Frank Pace, Jr.
Chief Executive Officer,
International Executive
Service Corps

Senior Professional Staff
Donald A. Hicks

TABLE OF
Contents

Chapter 1

Perspective ON Urban America
FOR THE EIGHTIES

T he social and economic forces that shape and sustain our nation's communities, and the circumstances that define life in them, are potent and enduring. These myriad forces operate in concert with the flow of population, whose rate of growth, composition, and patterns of redistribution influence the form and function of an array of societal institutions, including family, school, government, business, and the city—all of which represent continuing efforts to manage, if not to solve, perennial problems. Although these forces and the institutional traces left in their wakes hold their own fascination, the city and the urban cultures that define its changing form and function are the focus of this report, prepared by the Panel on Policies and Prospects for Metropolitan and Nonmetropolitan America, of the President's Commission for a National Agenda for the Eighties.

The Emergence of Postindustrial Urban America

A major societal transformation, particularly evident since World War II, has been unfolding in this nation, causing urban and rural America to experience change at unprecedented rates. The populations of central cities in the larger and older metropolitan areas have been shrinking rapidly, while other communities have been experiencing rapid and unplanned growth. Retarded growth rates, and even actual declines, have been witnessed within older central cities, suburbs, metropolitan areas, and entire multistate regions, accompanied by a revival of growth in traditionally lagging regions, small towns, and rural areas far removed from metropolitan areas. Indeed, the major theme that serves as the backdrop for this report is the deconcentration trends unfolding at several spatial scales—jobs, people, capital, income, and the culture of city-based life have dispersed within and beyond cities, metropolitan areas, and multistate regions.

Because the changes are proceeding at a pace that makes adjustment often difficult and painful, these redistributions can easily be viewed as the *causes* of myriad forms of economic, fiscal, and social distress affecting

1

individuals and their institutions wherever they are located. However, the Panel believes that such a view is shortsighted and potentially misleading. These trends are more accurately viewed as the *consequences* of a powerful transformation that is gradually ushering this nation from the industrial era into the postindustrial era, which:

> . . . can be outlined schematically along five dimensions: the creation of a service economy; the preeminence of the professional and technical class; the centrality of theoretical knowledge as the source of innovation and policy formulation in society; the possibility of self-sustaining technological growth and transformation; and the emergence of a new intellectual technology [centering] on information and information-processing, leading to the growth of a quaternary [administration and control by information exchange] sector in the economy.[1]

The passage into postindustrial society is marked by concern for the inability of an increasing number of communities to compensate from within for their losses through outmigration of capital, manufacturing jobs, entire industries, and even the capacity for innovation itself that enabled cities to regenerate continuously throughout the industrial era. The changes within urban economies—whereby services once considered secondary to and dependent on manufacturing now constitute the backbone and chief export product of many urban and regional economies—have been accompanied by a wide range of secondary changes (such as the blurred distinction between business and government domains) that ripple through and affect all aspects of urban America.

The city is such a dominant force in urban society that envisioning its future role without being influenced by its historical role is difficult. The city is perceived as something that should be largely permanent and unchanging, reflecting continuity and stability, promising to be a lasting monument to society's achievements and failures, and serving as a testimony to the success with which people have hammered out relations among themselves.

What can too easily be lost sight of is the fact that cities are the result of a continual series of adjustments. They are the surest barometer of change in a society as population adjusts to a changing economic base, as the built environment adjusts to the natural environment, as industry adjusts to technological capacity, and as social expectations adjust to economic realities. Cities are the social and physical evidence of past collective choices; they reflect accommodations to the constraints posed by physical space and time; they represent social compacts among social groups and across generations. They should be allowed to change in step with widespread changes in the larger society. This report seeks to underscore the long-term inevitability and desirability of this transformation, whose effects are so clearly evident in settlements across the nation.

Generally, this transformation has become known by its current consequences rather than by its potential opportunities and advantages. The concentrated poverty, dependence, unemployment, fiscal imbalances, tax-base erosion, and deterioration of physical plants and public service infrastructures within hundreds of communities throughout the nation translate into distress and despair for many who find themselves "left behind" in cities. Understandably, there is little patience for abstractly accepting these instances of individual and institutional distress as unavoidable accompaniments of large-scale transformation. Throughout the report, however, the Panel has sought to understand these conditions in the context of our passage into a postindustrial era and to consider how that passage may be made with a minimal amount of distress.

The circumstances facing the nation's settlements can be viewed as the consequence of not only the long-term historical transformation, but also the declining performance of a traditionally strong U.S. economy in markets at home and abroad. By all conventional measures, the U.S. economy is in trouble; it too is transforming. Rates of economic growth are distressingly low, inflation and unemployment rates are stubbornly high and intractable, and the impact of a restructuring international marketplace is wrenching.

Urban Revitalization and National Economic Revitalization

The weakened functioning of the national economy aggravates, where it does not create, local individual and institutional distress. In earlier decades, gains for certain cities, regions, and social groups living within them did not typically imply losses to other places or groups. Today, the absence of strong and steady economic growth in the larger economy accentuates the results of the current redistributions, designating places and people living in them as either "winners" or "losers."

Urban revitalization is therefore critically dependent on economic revitalization. The health of the nation's communities cannot be isolated from the vitality of the larger economy. However, national economic policies that seek to increase productivity, to expand markets, to create jobs, and to nurture new industries also have the potential for conflict with urban revitalization efforts. Policies aimed at increasing the productivity and competitive position of industry (such as business tax cuts and accelerated depreciation allowances) may well lead to the outmigration of firms or to their secondary expansion away from distressed locations, where the costs of doing business are prohibitively high. Conversely, vigorous pursuit of a national urban policy—with its current emphasis on restoring economic vitality to distressed localities and regions—may undermine a more general effort to revitalize the national economy—with its relative deemphasis on what happens in specific places.

Can the goals of urban revitalization be made consonant with the goals of economic revitalization? Is it possible to pursue a concern for the fortunes of specific places, while at the same time showing concern for overall national economic performance? The Panel believes that this is possible, provided that the nation first reconsiders what is meant by "urban revitalization." If it is defined as the attempt to restore our older industrial cities and regions to the influential positions that they have held throughout the industrial era, urban revitalization shall surely fail, diminishing our prospects for a revitalized national economy. If, however, the nation is successful in striving to assist all urban centers to assume newer, more specialized social and economic roles, then our prospects for reconciling urban revitalization with national economic revitalization are encouraging.

To begin, certain understandings should be reached. An increasingly productive economy should be recognized as necessitating simultaneous painful growth and shrinkage, disinvestment and reinvestment, in communities throughout the nation. The redistributions resulting from the larger transformation of the economy and society will, of necessity, disadvantage certain places while they advantage others. The nation's settlements will have to undergo these adjustments, and their "health" will often have to be appreciated at new levels of population and employment.

The nation can no longer assume that cities will perform the full range of their traditional functions for the larger society. They are no longer the most desirable settings for living, working, or producing. They should be allowed to transform into more specialized service and consumption centers within larger urban economic systems. The Panel believes that this nation should reconcile itself to these redistribution patterns and should seek to discover in them opportunities to do new things well and old things better.

In contemporary urban America, both people and places suffer as places transform in step with a changing economy. However, the primary responsibility of the federal government is to assist people, and to do so as directly as possible. The nation should be skeptical of narrowly defined, local economic development efforts, which have been associated with the promise of restoring vitality to a wide variety of local communities as if each were a self-contained entity. Aiding places and local governments directly for the purpose of aiding people indirectly is a policy emphasis that should be reexamined at a time when successes are so few and public resources are so meager. The causal logic is intriguing, and indeed examples of success cannot be ignored. However, given the diversity of local circumstances, the exportability of policy approaches from one setting to another is highly questionable.

The Panel strongly agrees that localities should strive to maintain a strong and diversified economic base, as well as the institutions of local governance that enable them to meet their assigned responsibilities. As national treasures, cities have the right to expect certain kinds of assistance from higher levels of government. However, the Panel suggests that the principal role of the federal government should be to assist communities in adjusting to redistributional trends, rather than to attempt to reverse them. Ultimately, the federal government's concern for national economic vitality should take precedence over the competition for advantage among communities and regions.

Further, the fortunes of numerous poor and unskilled urban residents of cities are often largely unaffected by even healthy expansion within local economies. Therefore, greater direct assistance should be provided for these casualties of urban transformation. This assistance should focus on improving the access of people to economic opportunity, which can be achieved in several ways: by upgrading the unskilled through manpower development efforts so that existing local job opportunities can be exploited, by removing barriers to mobility that prevent people from migrating to locations of economic opportunity, and by providing migration assistance to those who wish and need it. People-to-jobs strategies, whether by retraining or relocation or both, should receive the same degree of emphasis that is now reserved for jobs-to-people strategies.

After two decades of federal policies with explicit urban objectives, it is an appropriate time to reassess contemporary policy aims in light of our current understanding of the nation's urban problems. New perspectives on what is happening to the nation's urban and rural communities, and why, will likely be more important than the creation of new policy tools designed expressly to accomplish more effectively policy aims that may no longer be appropriate. Are the circumstances defined as "problems" really prob-

A Federal Response to Urban Transformation: New Perspectives

lems? Do the transformations that create real problems require a policy arsenal arrayed against them? As the decade begins, discovering the difference between what should or should not be undertaken, what can and cannot be accomplished, by the federal government should receive careful consideration.

A federal policy approach to urban and rural America should reflect an appreciation of the abilities and limitations of public policy in a complex and changing world. A uniform and centrally administered urban policy cannot prevent or eliminate changing circumstances and resultant distress experienced by cities. Instead, a locality's ability to cope successfully with changes that it cannot control depends on its flexibility. Clear thinking about what the federal government should refrain from doing in urban policy is as critical as what it should begin or continue doing.

This Panel report does not seek to offer a single, coherent, and unified policy package for ameliorating the afflictions suffered by people and places in urban and rural America. To attempt to do so would be to blind ourselves to the more important lessons that experiences of the past two decades can bequeath to the decade ahead. A unified and coherent national urban policy designed to solve the problems of the nation's communities and those who live in them is not possible. Because a national urban policy is expected to be responsive to diverse cities, counties, metropolitan and nonmetropolitan areas, states, regions, and the people who live in all communities across the nation, it is hobbled from the start. No comprehensive national urban policy can be the tool to resolve all the conflicts among these entities. Ironically, a national urban policy is likely to generate as much conflict as it eliminates, simply because it is a political document that must be all things to all people and all places.

What this report does offer is a perspective from which the problems and prospects for urban and rural America in the coming decade may be viewed. The ongoing transformation of the nation's cities is examined in Chapter 2. Emphasis is given to the fact that the crises experienced by cities, although undesirable, are a normal concomitant of the functions that they perform for the larger society, rather than evidence of their decline and imminent "death." Cities are shown to be evolving in step with the larger society and economy. Thus, the kind and severity of distress that cities experience is dictated largely by their social and technological "age." This chapter discusses how the city, as it transforms, has gradually lost much of its capacity to perform certain historical functions, including the assimilation of immigrants and the provision of employment for unskilled residents. The emergence of an urban underclass, whose plight demands the best efforts of the public and private sectors, is viewed not as a symptom of urban decline but as a side effect of urban transformation.

The logic, dynamics, and consequences of economic and demographic deconcentration at several spatial scales—cities, suburbs, nonmetropolitan areas, multistate regions—is the major theme of Chapter 3. Whether or not regional convergence will be achieved is addressed, and the myth of "regentrification" and "rebirth" of cities is debated. Finally, the wisdom of rebuilding the nation's cities from historical social and economic blueprints is reassessed.

The economic consequences of industrial disinvestment for specific localities and the resulting fiscal consequences for local governments are addressed in Chapter 4. With regard to economic distress, the importance of the local noneconomic business climate for retaining and expanding economic enterprise and the limited efficacy of local economic development efforts to forestall or to compensate for disinvestment are discussed. The nature of local fiscal distress is examined, and the prospects for balancing local responsibilities with local resources by adjusting municipal service packages is addressed. Finally, the roles of state governments and the federal government and an expanded role for the private sector—especially for fiscal distress due to rapid growth—are considered.

In Chapter 5, the distress experienced by people, as opposed to places and their local governments, is examined. Social distress accompanies our nation's transformation to a service-dominated economy, because employment prospects for unskilled workers are progressively diminished and because existing job opportunities have migrated away from central cities and older regions. Although linking people to economic opportunity can be accomplished in many different ways, the chapter stresses the importance of assisting people to take advantage of opportunities, wherever they may exist. People-to-jobs approaches, involving both relocation through assisted migration efforts for those who wish to participate and training for the unskilled and retraining for the displaced worker, are emphasized. A case is made for reducing the jobs-to-people emphasis at the center of current local economic development strategies and in the existing national urban policy and for tailoring job creation efforts to those locations where they are most likely to succeed.

Although the federal-local relationship is a legitimate focus in urban policy and should be preserved in the coming decade, Chapter 6 considers ways in which states can become more involved in the intergovernmental partnerships required to meet urban policy objectives. The increasing sophistication and sensitivity of state governments to their roles in national issues recommend them as important policy partners for the future.

Contemporary federal urban policy and its orientations and capabilities are explored in Chapter 7. Relative policy emphases and the tools available to implement them are evaluated in light of the larger trends discussed above. In addition, the urban impacts of nonurban federal policies are considered. These analyses lead to a reassessment of the purpose and substance of the national urban policy, and suggestions are offered to aid in the differentiation between needed transitional and long-term policy actions and goals.

Chapter 8 examines what interim steps can be taken while a long-term federal urban policy approach is developed. Because fundamental problems with the operation of the federal system in all policy areas also have consequences for urban policy areas, decongesting the overloaded intergovernmental system is discussed as a method of regaining control over the manner in which levels of government interrelate within our federal system. Achieving greater coordination among current federal community and economic development efforts is also considered as a means of recognizing, if not rectifying, policy gaps, overlaps, and inconsistencies. Finally, the merits of considering the reassignment of traditional governmental functions among levels of government and between government and the private sector are considered.

In the final chapter, the new perspectives on urban America presented throughout this report are developed into an agenda of key urban policy issues that should be debated by the nation during the 1980s. The utility of a national urban policy and a redefinition of the proper federal role in the urban policy arena are discussed. How state and local governmental roles articulate with a newly defined federal role likewise is addressed. Finally, federal commitment to a locationally sensitive urban policy is weighed against the pressing need for revamped federal economic and social policies.

This report is a statement of emphases rather than explicit choices. It asserts that the potential conflicts between urban revitalization and economic revitalization can be resolved, provided that new definitions of the "problems," the "solutions," and the criteria for "success" are adopted. It acknowledges that local communities have been and will continue to be buffeted by developments that are less and less within their power to control. Accordingly, it seeks to sketch a more appropriate urban policy role for the federal government in the decade ahead.

The Panel hopes to confront the reader with the necessity of understanding contemporary urban and rural problems in the broader context of the emergence of a postindustrial society and economy, and of making federal policy efforts consonant with long-term developments rather than hypersensitive to immediate conditions and political pressures. However, a national policy role of active anticipation and adjustment should not be confused with passive acceptance of or resignation to an inescapable future. It is, rather, a call for policy interventions that are consistent with and complementary to large-scale economic and social transformations so that precious public and private resources are used where they have some chance of realizing lasting success. Ameliorating the impacts on people and places of the passage into a post-industrial America is a fitting and proper role for the federal government to assume in the decade ahead.

Federal urban policy has shown a curious evolution in the past 50 years. In responding to the Depression, early federal efforts directed toward cities were consistent with then current economic and demographic trends—the in-migration of people to economic opportunity in the city. However, as the industrial era in America began to wane and as jobs and people began to migrate out of the city, federal urban policy failed to keep pace with these trends. Consequently, as the 1980s begin, the nation finds itself reinforcing an outdated policy perspective. In the past two decades, federal policies have sought to preserve the functions inherited and the scale achieved by cities, rather than to assist them in adjusting to an emerging postindustrial era. Now is the time to begin a reassessment of what should be the proper federal role in urban policy for the decade ahead. Through this report, the Panel seeks to contribute to that effort.

1. B. J. L. Berry, *The Human Consequences of Urbanization: Divergent Paths in the Urban Experience of the Twentieth Century* (New York: St. Martin's Press, 1973), pp. 49-50.

Note

Berry, B. J. L. *The Human Consequences of Urbanization: Divergent Paths in the Urban Experience of the Twentieth Century.* New York: St. Martin's Press, 1973.

Byrom, F. L. "Towards an Industrial Strategy for the United States," testimony before the Subcommittee on the City, Committee on Banking, Finance, and Urban Affairs, U.S. House of Representatives, Washington, D.C., 1980.

Chinitz, B., ed. *Central City Economic Development.* Cambridge: Abt Books, 1979.

Choate, P. "Urban Revitalization and Industrial Policy: The Next Steps," testimony before the Subcommittee on the City, Committee on Banking, Finance, and Urban Affairs, U.S. House of Representatives, Washington, D.C., 1980.

Congressional Quarterly, Inc. *Urban America: Policies and Problems.* Washington, D.C.: Congressional Quarterly, Inc., 1978.

Glickman, N. J., ed. *The Urban Impacts of Federal Policies.* Baltimore: Johns Hopkins University Press, 1980.

Goldsmith, W. W. and Derian, M. J. "Toward a National Urban Policy— Critical Reviews, Is There an Urban Policy?" *Journal of Regional Science.* Vol. 19, No. 1 (1979):93-108.

Graham, O. L., Jr. *Toward a Planned Society: From Roosevelt to Nixon.* London: Oxford University Press, 1976.

Hirschhorn, L. "Toward a National Urban Policy—Critical Reviews, The Urban Crisis: A Post-Industrial Perspective," *Journal of Regional Science.* Vol. 19, No. 1 (1979):109-118.

Howell, J. M. "Urban Revitalization and Industrial Policy," testimony before the Subcommittee on the City, Committee on Banking, Finance, and Urban Affairs, U.S. House of Representatives, Washington, D.C., 1980.

The President's Urban and Regional Policy Group, U.S. Department of Housing and Urban Development. *A New Partnership to Conserve America's Communities: A National Urban Policy.* Washington, D.C.: U.S. Government Printing Office, 1978.

Schwartz, G. G. *Retrospect and Prospects: An Urban Policy Profile of the United States.* Columbus, Ohio: The Academy for Contemporary Problems, 1979.

Schwartz, G. G. "Urban Revitalization and Industrial Policy: The Issues," testimony before the Subcommittee on the City, Committee on Banking, Finance, and Urban Affairs, U.S. House of Representatives, Washington, D.C., 1980.

Solomon, A. P., ed. *The Prospective City: Economic, Population, Energy, and Environmental Developments Shaping Our Cities and Suburbs.* Cambridge: The MIT Press, 1980.

Subcommittee on the City, Committee on Banking, Finance, and Urban Affairs, U.S. House of Representatives, 95th Congress, First Session. *Toward a National Urban Policy.* Washington, D.C.: U.S. Government Printing Office, 1977.

Thurow, L. C. *The Zero-Sum Society: Distribution and the Possibilities for Economic Change.* New York: Basic Books, 1980.

U.S. Department of Housing and Urban Development. *The President's National Urban Policy Report.* Washington, D.C.: U.S. Government Printing Office, 1978.

U.S. Department of Housing and Urban Development. *The President's National Urban Policy Report.* Washington, D.C.: U.S. Government Printing Office, 1980.

References

10

Chapter 2

THE **City** IN
Transition

*We did not, for the most part, build great cities in
this country; manufacturing firms agglomerated
in tight industrial complexes and formed labor
pools of half a million workers.* That is not the
same thing as building great cities. We sort of
woke up one day and there was Cleveland. There
was Detroit, with four [and] a half million people,
the biggest factory town on earth. *Our great
industrial transformation has left us with a large
number of overgrown "cities"—a ramification we
have not faced up to.*[1]

This nation has never fully come to grips with the
social and economic importance of its central
cities. They have seldom been fully appreciated
as the wellspring of our power and wealth since
the Industrial Revolution. Central cities have seldom been
recognized as generating health and welfare for generations of residents and wave after wave of immigrants. Central cities have seldom been noted as the crossroads for
new ideas, the residence of specialists, the incubators for
new economic activities, the distributors of opportunity,
and the homes of millions of families. Instead, our culture
has often viewed central cities and life in them as something to be suffered and endured, but certainly not fitting
subjects of national adoration, as is the case for certain
older European cities. As urban America has displaced
rural America, the most common cultural response has
been a recitation of what has been lost, rather than what
has been gained.

Likewise, this nation has never acknowledged the principal characteristics of cities that make them such valuable
assets—their status as both cause and consequence of
change, and their ability to mirror and magnify both promises and problems of the larger society. Their continued
strength is always tied to their ability to accept and
accommodate change within their physical forms and civic
functions. A nation that cannot appreciate why cities are

11

here, what they do, and that they must change in order to survive and to remain valuable is a nation that may well misperceive the changes that cities face in the future.

America's cities, and particularly those that experienced rapid growth during the 19th century, are less conscious creations than accumulations—the products of ongoing change. As the locus of the crises and tensions associated with the larger forces shaping society, they have and will continue to transform. Change is seldom a fluid and unencumbered process, and the transformation of America's cities is conditioned by two factors: their current lifestage and their historical legacy of functions. The result of transformation is a changing role for central cities—from centers of manufacturing to centers of service production and consumption. Finally, a major consequence of their changing role is the creation of an urban underclass of the poor and the dependent.

The city, by its very nature, is the locus of crisis for a society:

Crisis in the City

> In the Western World, the city has been almost continually in crisis. . . . The recurring crises are symptomatic of the profound revolution in man's way of living that has been in the making for a number of centuries. . . . In the nature of things, cities stand at the vortices of the currents and crosscurrents of broad-scale changes that alter and reconstitute societies. It is to be expected, therefore, that the intermittent eruptions incidental to the uneven course of change should exert their most violent effects at these centers.[2]

Crisis in cities should not be considered unusual. Cities function to solve problems. However, a city is a problem-generating as well as a problem-solving institution. Its concentrated and complex social and economic arrangements often result in problems of insufficient or inadequate housing, crime, congestion, pollution, and so forth. In addition, what constitutes a remedy for one person or group may well constitute a problem for others.

Despite the long list of problems identified with the city, its culture has generated more health, wealth, and welfare for its residents than nonurban arrangements. Yet, the shortcomings of a society, as well as its achievements, are nowhere more apparent than they are in its cities. The city provides an opportunity not only to observe existing inequalities, but also to ignore them. Where observed, urban culture provides both the logic explaining their existence and the critical mass of sentiment that can lead to reducing them.

"Cities, like people, pass through life-cycles during which their values and functions change."[3] The dynamic underlying this developmental process is biological only by analogy, however. The sequence of stages through which cities pass as they "age" may be defined by their changing functions and capacities to produce and to distribute goods and services; passage through these stages is better tracked on a technological than on a calendrical timeline.

Cities may be usefully categorized by age or lifestage, demarcated by the dates at which they reached critical population thresholds. For example, New York City reached the population threshold of 350,000 just before 1840; Philadelphia just before 1860; Washington, D.C., just before 1920; and Dallas in the early 1940s. Such lifestage distinctions sensitize us to the fact that American cities have emerged and matured during different historical eras. The social and economic functions that cities perform for their citizens, their regions, and the nation vary, depending where on the technological timeline a city's birth and growth are tied to. In North America, the more recently a city has experienced the bulk of its growth, the lower its overall density is likely to be. This situation occurs largely because most 20th-century technological progress has loosened the ties of people and activities to a common location or to one another.

Mature cities serve as artifacts that illustrate physically the evolution of society's technological capabilities. For example, the older cities in the Northeast and upper Midwest (hereafter referred to as the Industrial Heartland) have a spatial arrangement that reflects reaching maturity during an essentially industrial era. Factories, retail and service centers, housing, streets, and public service infrastructures (the resources to provide and to administer services) were combined in compact and concentrated arrangements to accommodate the requirements of the prevailing modes of production technology and the state of the art in transportation and communication. Industrial cities such as Boston, Cleveland, and Detroit stand as "bricks-and-mortar" snapshots of a bygone era. Subsequent change, therefore, is conditioned by these legacies.

Many older cities in this nation, faced with declining population and economic vitality, stand as "withering monuments to the industrial age."[4] In many respects, they are 19th-century forms functioning in a 20th-century America. Constructed to house the industrial engines of the 19th-century urban economy, as well as a labor pool stratified by ethnicity, class, religion, later race, and a host of other

13

differences, the linkage between urban location and urban life was established. One could have continual access to city life and its amenities only by locating in a city.

Technological advances in long-distance transportation and communication, including rail, road, and telegraph systems, gradually knitted the nation's communities into an integrated system. The resulting pattern, which bound small towns and large cities together, reflected a hierarchy of specialized places and regional and industrial divisions of labor that increasingly lent coherence and vitality to the nation as a whole.

During the 20th century, technological advances in short-distance transportation and communication had a similar effect within cities—expanding the scope of urban activities, extending the culture of the city to the surrounding countryside, and enhancing the access of households and firms to others elsewhere in the city. The concentration of people and their activities, however, made accessibility within cities more difficult to achieve than accessibility between cities.

During this century, distinctive social and economic patterns emerged, reflecting the changing internal structure of the city. Activities such as residence, commerce, and manufacturing no longer required concentration in a common location. Groups and functions could use physical space to sort themselves out over the urban landscape. As city populations grew to include more residents characterized by a broad range of differences, people and economic activities could increasingly cluster on the basis of similarities. Households began to sort themselves by income, race-ethnicity, and occupational differences. Likewise, residence could be separated from workplace, production from administration, and so forth. Consequently, as the 19th century gave way to the 20th century, the linkage between urban location and urban life began to unravel. Increasingly, people could live an essentially urban life without residing in the city, primarily because technology had made the city and its amenities ever more accessible to nearly everyone.

Over the decades of the 20th century, people, their jobs, and their allegiances have departed the inner city for the periphery and beyond, to live at lower densities and in the presence of others like themselves. As a result of advancing technological capabilities, urban life can increasingly be experienced over an expanded territory. The larger older cities have been transforming continually because the dynamism of urban life increasingly spills out beyond their borders. In the process, the historical legacies of physical arrangements evident within cities condition their transformation and their ability to adjust to changing circumstances.

Comprehending the city in terms of the long-term developmental sweep of history aids in imparting an appreciation of its historical roles in society: provision of public services (for example, sewage, water, sanitation, traffic control); education and training opportunities; public health facilities; recreation resources; housing; markets for goods; and acculturation and assimilation of immigrants.

Today, many cities are experiencing increased difficulty in performing their historical roles. The dispersal of economic activity and consequent population loss leave a preponderance of marginal industries and low-income households in the cities. Nonetheless, the "death of the city" is not at hand. The city is transforming and its roles are changing. In the future, it will perform a narrower range of increasingly specialized functions for the larger urban society. However, acceptance of changing roles has been slow, even though the continued dominance of cities in our culture is not seriously questioned. The city, with its historical form and functions, can command so much attention that it is difficult to appreciate that it will and should change or to imagine what the city in the future will be like.

The nation's cities are transforming from centers of material goods production to centers of service consumption. "The era of massive centralized industrialization is over and . . . large, dense concentrations of people and firms have become technologically obsolete."[5] Yet, special efforts to lure manufacturing industries back to older central cities continue as the principal aim of innumerable economic development efforts sponsored by municipalities and states. Support at the local level is only hesitantly directed at developing the old central core of cities in terms of their remaining considerable competitive strengths. Indeed, certain types of economic activity, particularly those that benefit from centrality and high-density arrangements, continue to belong in the central cities and may be encouraged by incentives. The health and vitality that could result is not easily acknowledged, because this transformation is often accompanied by a shrinking population that includes ever higher proportions of the poor and the dependent—those who make the most frequent and costly claims on local governments.

The current surge in service sector growth (reflected in office construction), a demand for middle-class housing leading to limited neighborhood upgrading, and the demand for recreation and entertainment facilities are signs of a new central city vitality that will continue to transform the city, even if this revitalization is not in preparation for a return to what the city once was. "The cores of our central cities should be revitalized as culturally rich, architecturally exciting magnets for conventions, tourism, and leisure time pursuits of regional, national and

15

even international populations."[6] This direction promises the most potential for central city economic expansion and job generation for the rest of the century.

What will the city transform into? Office jobs for well paid white-collar managerial, professional, financial, and knowledge-class occupations will increase. As a result, a variety of allied services that these people and their employing institutions demand during and after working hours will be required. Blue-collar jobs will be reduced because of the continued outmigration of blue-collar employment to noncentral locations. The general decline in rural in-migration may allow the city to relinquish its traditional function of acculturating and assimilating newcomers to urban life. However, a rising tide of foreign immigrants—especially from the Caribbean perimeter—may shift the task of accommodation and assimilation to a few selected cities. Cities will become scaled-down residential centers for an array of households, defined by a narrower range of age, household composition, and income differences. Finally, the older industrial cities will become more specialized national and regional centers, primarily performing business, service, finance, and governmental functions.

The city probably will evolve to the point where its physical form and spatial arrangement become more perfectly articulated with its new roles. This transformation should neither cause alarm nor impel actions to counter the long-term and extremely powerful demographic, economic, and technological forces at work. Policymakers should neither seek to restore the industrial city to its former form and functions, nor force urban society to perform tasks in ways and in locations that are no longer appropriate.

Throughout history, the nation's cities have attracted and accommodated wave after wave of poor immigrants, both from abroad and from the rural hinterland. As city populations grew, the city's major social functions became increasingly evident: upgrading housing, health, and employment prospects for the majority, while acculturating succeeding streams of immigrants.

The new arrivals, and especially their children, acquired the necessary skills to move themselves into the social and economic mainstream. However, immigrants from varied and diverse backgrounds were not being culturally homogenized, even though their cultural differences increasingly could exist in a common physical, if not social, space. Ethnic and religious cultural diversity survived and was continually reflected in clustered neighborhoods and communities. During this time, America

The City in Transition and the Urban Underclass

16

adopted the "melting pot" metaphor, an imagery that obscured the persistence of the "social stew," which more accurately characterizes city-based society.

For decades, the acculturation dynamic functioned reasonably well for most new arrivals, enabling them and their children to join an increasingly diverse middle class. However, as the city has transformed to adjust to the changing economic, demographic, and technological realities, it has become less able to perform this historical social role. The result has been the creation of an urban underclass—the poor and the dependent (overly represented by youth, elderly, unskilled).

Two basic factors account for this functional failure. First, the city's capacity to perform the processing task has deteriorated because of cultural responses to certain characteristics ascribed to the *people*, particularly racial and ethnic minorities, who are predominately located in central cities. Minorities have more difficulty in achieving assimilation into the social and economic mainstream. The bulwark against this change has been the historical legacy of slavery and the contemporary effects of race-conscious *de jure* (explicit discrimination in laws) followed by *de facto* mechanisms (unofficial biases) that have allocated advantage, opportunity, and security differentially in our society.

With regard to white ethnic urban poor, historically few insurmountable barriers to assimilation and general acceptance stood in their way. They could move up and on once educational and employment opportunities were provided. For racial minorities, however, the social and economic escalators did not function as effectively. Access to traditional avenues to success were blocked by individual and institutional discrimination, as well as by the dispersal of economic opportunity to places outside central cities. Although the assimilation process had enabled earlier immigrants or their offspring to use the city as a launching pad, a growing proportion of poor blacks and Hispanics has been left behind, and sizeable proportions have become part of a nearly permanent urban underclass.

A second factor in the breakdown of the cities' capacity to perform this traditional role relates to certain characteristics ascribed to particular *places,* particularly older industrial cities. The city no longer can generate diffuse social and economic well-being for all of its residents. The city has lost much of its capacity to provide upgrading opportunities for the poor and to send them along—either upward through successive social strata or outward to alternative locations where economic opportunities exist in relative abundance. This situation is true largely because the city can no longer generate the jobs needed by its unskilled young and poor residents. Not only the number of jobs in certain cities has shrunk, but also the mix of jobs has been transformed—from high proportions of unskilled manufacturing jobs to high proportions of skilled jobs in the manufacturing and service sectors. These latter jobs are often mismatched—although evidence for this is by no means definitive—to an urban underclass that largely consists of minority and youthful residents. Minority males, in particular, are the most severely mismatched with the available job prospects. Many cities have often become the last stop, rather than a stopping point, for the contemporary urban underclass.

Although the living standards of poor people generally improved during the 1960s, poverty, whether defined officially by absolute criteria or socially by relative criteria, has persisted. Today, much poverty has been redistributed—from the rural hinterland to the shrinking older industrial cities of the Northeast and Midwest. The corresponding decline of poverty in nonmetropolitan places, which benefitted both poor blacks and poor whites, was the result less of people migrating out of rural areas than of economic vitality migrating in. The South in particular has been the recipient of an influx of economic vitality, benefitting large numbers of poor southerners.

Between 1970 and 1978, a net outmigration from metropolitan areas of 2.7 million people took place. Between 1962 and 1978, 56 percent of all new manufacturing jobs were established outside metropolitan areas, with 30 percent locating in the nonmetropolitan South alone. Coincident with these trends, the nation's poverty population came to include an increasing number of blacks. Although the number of whites experiencing poverty situations declined by 250,000 between 1969 and 1977, the number of poor blacks rose by 600,000. In 1959, blacks constituted 26 percent of the nation's poor; in 1969, 29 percent; by 1977, 31 percent.

The number of poor central city blacks has grown over the past two decades. After a slight decline (from 3.8 million in 1959 to 3.1 million in 1969), the number of poor central city blacks grew to 4.3 million by 1977—an increase of nearly 40 percent during the seventies. The separate fate of the white population is illustrated by the fact that the number of poor whites did not increase during the same period. The unemployment figures for minority young men (20 to 24 years old) doubled (from 10 percent to 20 percent) between 1965 and 1978. Among minority teenagers, the 1978 rates exceeded 30 percent—twice as high as those for the mid-1950s. Some observers have concluded that there is no general problem of youth unemployment—only one for young blacks.

Although only a relatively small proportion of the U.S. population (approximately 5 percent) endures urban residential circumstances that constitute what is often called a "ghetto," the significance of this stratum belies its numerical size. Because traditional economic opportunities have been migrating out of cities for so long, the urban poor left behind are increasingly distressed. Income and employment differentials between this stranded group and the rest of society have increased. Furthermore, the turn-over rate is not nearly as high as has been the case historically. Therefore, the condition of a sizeable portion of the urban underclass is relatively permanent. Avenues of escape are shrinking, unreliable, and inadequate.

The context of the ghetto may provide an explanation for the permanence of the conditions afflicting the minor-ity urban underclass. The ghetto constitutes a massive barrier to the larger society and a concentration of disad-vantages that militate against individuals and their insti-tutions. This concentrative aspect and the multiple subtle interactions between the barrier and disadvantages defines the ghetto as a social context:

> Many minority children . . . living in neighbor-hoods where few people who do go to work regularly have much to show for it, see little point in taking school seriously or believing it can help to get a job that will lead anywhere. If their early job history and work experience confirm their pessimistic expectations, many give up. . . . The poor experience . . . during their late adolescence and young adulthood leaves them permanently disadvantaged.[7]

Because the national economy is evolving in concert with the arrival of the postindustrial era, our major cities, in particular, will be required to assume new, more special-ized, economic roles. In the process, their historical capac-ities to assimilate and upgrade an urban underclass are effectively diminished. Although nearly continuous urban crisis is a part of a city's nature because its economic and social functions can never be perfectly meshed, the result-ing distress experienced by its residents cannot be viewed as acceptable. Therefore, a proper focus of wise urban policy is to alleviate that distress in ways that have long-term prospects for success.

1. W. Thompson, "Economic Processes and Employment Problems in Declining Metropolitan Areas," in *Post-Industrial America: Metropolitan Decline and Inter-Regional Job Shifts,* eds., G. Sternlieb and J. W. Hughes (New Brunswick, N.J.: Center for Urban Policy Research, 1975), p. 189. (Emphasis supplied.)
2. A. H. Hawley, *Urban Society: An Ecological Approach* (New York: Ronald Press, 1971), p. 3.
3. J. Q. Wilson, "The War on Cities," *The Public Interest,* 3 (Spring 1966), reprinted in *The Modern City: Readings in Urban Economics,* eds., D. W. Rasmussen and C. T. Haworth (New York: Harper & Row, 1973), p. 24.
4. G. Sternlieb and J. W. Hughes, "The New Economic Geography of America," in *Revitalizing the Northeast: Prelude to an Agenda,* eds., G. Sternlieb and J. W. Hughes (New Brunswick, N.J.: Center for Urban Policy Research, 1978), p. 115.
5. J. D. Kasarda, "The Implications of Contemporary Redistribution Trends for National Urban Policy," paper contributed to the President's Commission for a National Agenda for the Eighties, Washington, D.C.: 1980, p. 31. (Forthcoming in *Social Science Quarterly,* December 1980.)
6. Ibid., p. 32.
7. E. Ginzberg, "Youth Unemployment," *Scientific American,* Vol. 242, No. 5 (May 1980):47.

Notes

Berry, B. J. L. *The Human Consequences of Urbanization: Divergent Paths in the Urban Experience of the Twentieth Century.* New York: St. Martin's Press, 1973.

Berry, B. J. L. "Inner City Futures: An American Dilemma Revisited," *Transactions.* London: Institute of British Geographers (1980):1-28.

Blair, J. P. "The Changing Economics of the Urban Promise." Washington, D.C.: Office of Evaluation, U.S. Department of Housing and Urban Development, undated draft paper.

Bollens, J. C. and Schmandt, H. J. *The Metropolis: Its People, Politics, and Economic Life.* New York: Harper & Row, 1975.

Fossett, J. W. and Nathan, R. P. "The Prospects for Urban Revival," in *Urban Government Finances in the 1980s.* ed., Roy Bahl. Beverly Hills: Sage Publications, forthcoming.

Goldfield, D. R. and Brownell, B. A. *Urban America: From Downtown to No Town.* Boston: Houghton Mifflin Company, 1979.

Goodman, J. L., Jr. *Urban Residential Mobility: Places, People, and Policy.* Washington, D.C.: The Urban Institute, 1978.

Graff, H. J. "Culture and the City; Culture in the City: Is There a Relationship?" paper contributed to the President's Commission for a National Agenda for the Eighties, Washington, D.C., 1980.

Hawley, A. H. *Urban Society: An Ecological Approach.* New York: Ronald Press, 1971.

Hawley, A. H. and Rock, V. P., eds. *Metropolitan America: In Contemporary Perspective.* New York: John Wiley & Sons, Inc., Halsted Press; Sage Publications, Inc., 1975.

Kasarda, J. D. "The Implications of Contemporary Redistribution Trends for National Urban Policy," paper contributed to the President's Commission for a National Agenda for the Eighties, Washington, D.C. and forthcoming in *Social Science Quarterly,* December 1980.

Long, L. H. and Dahmann, D. *The City-Suburb Income Gap: Is It Being Narrowed by a Back-to-the-City Movement?* Special Demographic Analyses, U.S. Bureau of the Census. Washington, D.C.: U.S. Government Printing Office, 1980.

Morrison, P., Vaughan, R., Vernez, G., and Williams, B. *Recent Contributions to the Urban Policy Debate.* Santa Monica: Rand Corporation, 1979.

References

Nathan, R. P. and Fossett, J. W. "Urban Conditions: Implications for Federal Policy," *Commentary* (April 1979):3-7.

Norton, R. D. *City Life-Cycles and American Urban Policy.* New York: Academic Press, Inc., 1979.

Solomon, A. P., ed. *The Prospective City: Economic, Population, Energy, and Environmental Developments Shaping Our Cities and Suburbs.* Cambridge: The MIT Press, 1980.

Sternlieb, G. and Hughes, J. W., eds. *Post-Industrial America: Metropolitan Decline and Inter-Regional Job Shifts.* New Brunswick, N.J.: Center for Urban Policy Research, 1975.

Sternlieb, G. and Hughes, J. W., eds. *Revitalizing the Northeast: Prelude to an Agenda.* New Brunswick, N.J.: Center for Urban Policy Research, 1978.

Subcommittee on the City, Committee on Banking, Finance, and Urban Affairs, U.S. House of Representatives, 95th Congress, First Session. *Toward a National Urban Policy.* Washington, D.C.: U.S. Government Printing Office, 1977.

U.S. Department of Housing and Urban Development. *A Survey of Citizens Views and Concerns about Urban Life.* Washington, D.C.: U.S. Government Printing Office, 1978.

Weinstein, B. L. and Clark, R. J. "Urban Trends and the Condition of Cities." Washington, D.C.: Southern Growth Policies Board, 1979, draft report.

Chapter 3

THE
Deconcentration OF
Urban America

I n our relatively short national history, the United States transformed from a predominately rural and agricultural nation into a predominately urban and industrial nation. That transformation has unfolded slowly, but relentlessly, decade after decade. Gradually, a new, equally important transformation trend has been discovered—the deconcentration of urban America.

The migration of people and industry from cities to the suburbs and beyond is the central theme explored in this chapter. The dynamics of deconcentration and the pattern and consequences of multiscale decentralization are addressed. In addition, the prospect of regional convergence, the illusion of urban renaissance, and the implications of low-density development are examined. Finally, the question of whether or not our central cities should be rebuilt to reflect their historical economic orientations is discussed.

Since World War II, a simultaneous deconcentration of population and industrial activity at several geographic scales in the United States has become especially evident. Consequently, people live in and work at lower densities within cities, while densities are increasing in places beyond city borders. The deconcentration of people and jobs results in urban activity crossing city borders, the more abstract boundaries of metropolitan areas, and even multistate regions. The emerging demographic and economic geography across the nation will increasingly be characterized by lower density industrial and residential settlements that are built around multiple points of concentration within and between metropolitan areas. The influence of central cities will be diminished as certain production, residential, commercial, and cultural functions disperse to places beyond them.

In demographic terms, continual dispersion within metropolitan areas is now accompanied by both a broader movement of people to the periphery of metropolitan areas

The Dynamics of Deconcentration

and a rural reconcentration. During the industrial era, the rural-to-urban and South-to-North migration streams provided the labor force needed by northern factories. Today that migration has all but ceased. Furthermore, certain population groups, such as northern urban blacks, are returning to the newer southern urban areas in record numbers.

In terms of economic activity, the economic and related technological conditions that led to industrially based urban centers are gradually being unraveled. Both established industry and the potential for industrial innovation that spawns new industry have dispersed away from central urban areas, away from the Industrial Heartland, and in certain cases, out of the United States entirely. Although large-scale employment outmigration preceded household outmigration, the chained sequence of people following jobs has been eclipsed by the more prominent tendency for population increases in suburbs and beyond to attract new and relocated employment growth. The changing economic order reflects developments in production technology, the role of economic market forces, the rise of sociocultural (quality-of-life) forces, and the reinforcing role of government policies.

The advantages of agglomeration and central location have been eroded by technological innovations and new production technologies that have given locational freedom to an ever wider array of industries. Transportation and communication technologies have reinforced this dispersal because physical proximity has been eclipsed by electronic proximity. Micro-miniaturization and automation in both manufacturing and service production processes have eroded the necessity for industrial plants to cluster together. Difficulty in accumulating capital, complex local bureaucratic procedures engendering time and economic costs, general congestion, and deterioration of a wide variety of amenities and delivered services have further reduced the attractiveness of central locations. Increasingly, firms and people have moved away not because they must, but because they can. When relocation or expansion decisions are made, new central locations are often avoided. The complexity and interdependence traditionally associated with urban life in cities are increasingly perceived as liabilities rather than assets.

With regard to market forces, central urban locations have lost much of their competitiveness to noncentral locations. The costs of doing business in the nation's older central cities are estimated to be 20 to 30 percent greater than in surrounding suburbs or nonmetropolitan areas. In addition, policies geared to whittle away at that cost differential to make central cities more competitive have generally not been successful. The relative costs attached to production have increased significantly for labor, land, transportation, energy, capital, and tax-supported municipal services, facilitating the trend toward deconcentration. For example, labor (the most significant production cost) accounts for over half of the cost in manufacturing and over 90 percent of the cost in labor-intensive service industries. Lower labor costs outside central cities and the Industrial Heartland, in part due to less unionization and less restrictive industrial regulations, have encouraged the dispersion of industrial activity.

The potency of purely economic factors governing location decisions has been diluted by noneconomic factors. Quality-of-life considerations have acted as magnets that draw footloose households and industry to locations increasingly distant from central locations. The advantages historically found only in concentrated central locations increasingly can be enjoyed in relatively dispersed, low-density settings.

Federal policies also have operated to abet and to reinforce industrial and residential dispersion. In most cases, any "anti-city" bias has been implicit and inadvertent. Federal taxation policy that encourages new construction rather than restoration; housing policy that directs growth via subsidies to the periphery of metropolitan areas and beyond; water, sewer, and other utility subsidies; and transportation policy that drastically lowers the costs of access between distant points are all examples of unintended "anti-city" impacts of federal policies.

Intraregional, Interregional, and International Deconcentration Trends

Deconcentration of population and industry across the boundaries of cities, metropolitan areas, and multistate regions involves basic redistribution patterns whose causes are interwoven. Two patterns are intraregional; a third pattern is interregional. A fourth pattern of deconcentration mainly involves economic movements on an international scale.

Intraregional Deconcentration. Of the two intraregional redistribution patterns, the most familiar one occurs at the smallest scale—suburbanization, which is the outmigration of people and jobs from central cities to suburbs at the periphery. As a result of this process, which began in earnest during the 1920s, the metropolitan area emerged as an increasingly significant, if unofficial, unit of analysis for understanding the local and regional structure of urban America. This dispersion within metropolitan areas continued through the 1970s. Recently, and for the first time in U.S. history, many larger, older metropolitan areas have experienced the shrinkage process that was once the fate only of older industrial cities.

Although more recent in origin, the second intraregional redistribution pattern—nonmetropolitan growth—is equally portentous in its consequences. Approximately half of the new nonmetropolitan growth is adjacent to existing metropolitan areas. This growth probably occurs because the boundary definition of certain metropolitan areas does not allow them to capture and to contain all of the economic and social vitality in the area. However, a roughly equal portion of nonmetropolitan growth is nonadjacent to and remote from existing metropolitan areas. Indeed, the nation's smallest places (nonurban settlements of less than 2,500 population) are the fastest growing today. The policy implications of growth in nonmetropolitan areas outpacing growth within metropolitan areas have only recently received serious consideration.

Within regions, both dispersal patterns bode ill for the maintenance of central cities' historical place in society. The dynamics of urban change are judged by some to be enervating central cities within all regions of the nation. The economic health within metropolitan areas but outside central cities has seldom been viewed as adequate compensation for central city shrinkage. The absolute decline in population and jobs (particularly those jobs that generate middle-range household incomes) in so many of the central cities that anchor major metropolitan areas has been unrelenting and powerful. As a result, serious doubt exists about the continued ability of these central cities to perform their wide variety of historical residential, production, and commercial functions. Whether or not this prognosis is necessarily undesirable should be given a great deal of consideration.

Interregional Deconcentration. A third pattern of redistribution is unfolding at the interregional scale. First the West (until about 1960) and now the South have emerged *seriatim* as the major growth centers of the nation. The dispersal pattern is occurring on a scale large enough to transcend entire multistate regions. Although the dynamics underlying deconcentration have been present for decades, their regional consequences have built up slowly. The interregional dispersion of jobs has occurred much faster than the redistribution of population. This process has been going on for decades without generating much concern in the Industrial Heartland, largely because employment losses from migration were continually compensated by the spawning of new industrial activity. Today, however, with most of these shifts probably completed, sectionalism has developed in response to the discovery of the dispersion trend, but this response is often based on a misperception. Most concern for the fate of the Industrial Heartland is focused on a largely uncritical reliance on relative growth rates examined across regions, rather than the absolute amount of economic vitality that exists within regions.

The Industrial Heartland is certainly not in a rapid state of decline. All regions of the country are growing in jobs, income per capita, and population. In terms of industrial expansion, personal income, retail sales, bank deposits, and construction starts (conventional measures of economic performance), the growth in the Industrial Heartland has been only relatively slower than that in other regions. In other words, some measure of regional convergence has been working within the national economy, but this might be heralded just as accurately as the South "catching up" as the North "stagnating" or "declining."

International Deconcentration. Another form of economic deconcentration of increasing importance is primarily of international significance, because it is occurring at the largest geographical scale—industrial activity crossing national borders. This large-scale deconcentration cannot easily be seen in zero sum terms for the United States. What is taking place is no longer simply a spatial rearrangement of advantages and disadvantages among people, places, and industrial sectors within the nation. Rather, the net costs attached to the loss of our comparative advantage in a number of industrial sectors within the international marketplace are substantial and accumulating.

Although American transnational investment patterns of the 1960s caused particular consternation within European nations, a reverse transnational investment in America by other countries began in the late 1970s. This international economic restructuring is stark testimony to the power and inevitability of the deconcentration forces at work. To a notable degree, a certain universality to the deconcentration process exists among the most technologically advanced nations. Furthermore, like the redistribution patterns within the nation's borders, the underlying dynamics have been operating for some time.

Countless analyses have inventoried the major negative implications of the deconcentration patterns at several geographic scales. Using the central city as a unit of analysis, the erosion of fiscal capacity, the increased ghettoization of the poor and minorities, the enduring high

Consequences of Multiscale Decentralization

27

unemployment rates, the chronic economic depression in poverty neighborhoods, the underuse of the built environment, the deterioration of urban public services and facilities, and the excessive use of resources per capita are all consequences traditionally associated with deconcentration, dispersion, and low-density social and economic arrangements.

Within the metropolitan area, the loss of economic and industrial vitality to nonmetropolitan areas has created far less anxiety, because metropolitan areas, for the most part, are not political realities but analytic constructs. However, many small towns and nonmetropolitan areas are woefully underprepared to handle their new growth. The pain and dislocation accompanying unplanned expansion can often be as unpleasant as that accompanying unplanned decline.

On a multistate regional scale, the situation is much the same. Interregional rates of demographic and economic growth have undergone change. If anything, the consequences have simply meant a lessening of the historical disparities that have existed among major regions of the country. These large-scale redistribution patterns should not be viewed as national problems, because past disparities are being lessened in favor of the chronically disadvantaged regions and their residents. With regard to the currently waning Sunbelt-Snowbelt sectional competition, the North remains dominant on all measures of economic performance and has lost ground to the South in relative terms only.

The consequences of ongoing international economic reordering are registered at all geographic scales within the nation. Cities, metropolitan areas, and even regions are awash with international economic trends and influences that national economic policy machinery seemingly can no longer completely control. The most obvious example is the decline in the U.S. automotive industry and allied industries such as steel and tires.

The cumulative consequences of deconcentration have become intimidating largely because the rate of the process makes the gradual adjustment by older urban forms (neighborhoods, cities, metropolitan areas, and even regions) difficult, if not impossible, to achieve. Change in itself is seldom much of a problem unless it occurs at a pace that prevents smooth adjustment.

A major consequence of dominant patterns of regional dispersion is that multistate regions are becoming more similar as historical social and economic gaps between them close. For all practical purposes, the truth of this assessment applies to the deconcentration and dispersal trends. As a result, the distinctions at all spatial scales—between urban and rural, central city and suburb, metropolitan and

Convergence and Renaissance: Unrealistic Expectations

nonmetropolitan, and even entire regions—have declined in significance. As units of analysis in urban policy formulation and analysis, traditional dichotomies have been rendered less distinct by the redistribution process within and beyond our national society and economy.

Although the long-term trend toward convergence has been unmistakable, the disparities at any one scale probably will never be so completely eroded as to initiate a reversal of the deconcentration processes that precipitated them. One often unstated implication of the convergence dynamic is that central cities that lose economic vitality to suburbs, metropolitan areas that lose economic vitality to nonmetropolitan and rural areas, and multistate regions that lose economic vitality to others will rebound as their business cost disadvantages are whittled away relative to rising cost environments in suburbs, nonmetropolitan areas, and faster growing regions. The dynamic suggests an ebb and flow that supposedly never permanently disadvantages any locality.

Experience suggests, however, that complete convergence may remain an unfulfilled expectation. Although cost advantages of peripheral locations have eroded since widespread decentralization began, full-scale renewal of industrial activity in the dispossessed central cities and core regions is not likely to materialize. In addition, equalization within metropolitan areas, between central cities and suburbs, or among regions may not lead to renaissance, but only to a narrower revitalization. As cost differences diminish, the locations that originally lost vitality may not return to their former advantaged positions, but rather may evolve into settings for newer, more specialized territorially based social and economic systems. The direction of this development is not reversal or evolutionary backtracking, but a continuation of developmental trends that constantly require our nation's settlements to play new roles for the larger society and economy.

The Illusion of Urban Renaissance

In recent years, the incipient rebirth of cities has been highly touted. A so-called "regentrification" process has been heralded as marking the return of the middle class and their incomes, clout, and allegiances to the city. Residential and civic rejuvenation could be expected to follow, early reports suggested. Although casual observation indicates that portions of central city neighborhoods are indeed experiencing a great deal of housing stock upgrading and restoration, the evidence is spread so thinly across a number of cities that it defies statistical detection. What statistics do reveal, however, is the continuing deterioration of living conditions and income levels in central cities. Signs of the ongoing transformation of central cities are being misread as signaling the reversal of the very trends that they represent.

Although it may be premature to dismiss the likelihood that an upgrading of selected blocks of inner-city housing may one day herald the return of the middle class, the available evidence argues strongly against this view:

1. The overwhelming flow of middle-class households during the 1970s has been out of, not into, the central cities. For every household with incomes exceeding $15,000 which entered central cities between March 1975 and March 1978, three households left. Between 1970 and 1978, this net outmigration resulted in a loss of nearly $65 billion in disposable personal income to the nation's cities.
2. Revitalization has occurred in only a fraction of any city's neighborhoods. Between 1968 and 1979, only one-half of 1 percent of the nearly 20 million housing units in cities have been affected by revitalizaton or restoration efforts.
3. In excess of 70 percent of the households residing in revitalized central city units were intra-city movers and not immigrants from outside the city.
4. The concentration of minorities and poverty level population in central cities is continuing to increase, both in absolute and proportional terms. Between 1970 and 1978, central cities lost nearly 4 million white residents while the central city black population increased by 542,000. During the same period, the total number of central city residents below the poverty level increased by 235,000 including a net increase of 441,000 blacks below the poverty level.
5. Substantial residential and commerical disinvestment continues to be active in almost all older, larger, central cities, and far exceeds reinvestment.
6. The growth of central business district office employment during the 1970s has not nearly compensated for central city losses of blue-collar jobs and jobs in the retail and wholesale sectors. While New York City experienced an expansion in white-collar professional, clerical, and managerial jobs during the 1970s, on the whole New York City lost 600,000 jobs with an estimated tax loss of $500 million.[1]

In summary, the dispersion of jobs, people, and taxable income—especially in the Northeast and upper Midwest regions—is not being mitigated by a selective return of the middle class to the central city. Spot signs of revitalization should be judged more accurately as the continuing redistribution and reconcentration of selected households and their advantages within the city—a dynamic consistent with, not counter to, the prevailing central city deconcentration trend.

Because the inner-city neighborhood revitalization movement began without explicit federal intervention, the possibility exists that any future governmental involvement may only lessen any future chances of success. Although certain low-income households undoubtedly have been forced to relocate because of upgrading, this pattern is invariably part of inner-city rejuvenation. In any event, the extent of displacement has been overstated. Where it exists, care should be taken not to define displacement in a manner that leads to policies aimed at preventing what is also desirable inner-city upgrading. Such policy would have a chilling effect on spontaneous private reinvestment initiatives in our city centers. Sensitivity to the housing needs of low-income and elderly city residents could be better shown by assisting them to gain access to the transforming housing market rather than by implementing policies aimed at preventing displacement.

Reassessing Urban Sprawl and the Implications of Lower Density Development

Aside from impressionistic language suggesting the imminent demise of the city, the clearest illustration of the power of language symbols to cloud thinking about urban circumstances is the persistent concern about "urban sprawl." This notion is so firmly fixed in conventional wisdom that generating interest in analyzing it has been difficult at times. A thing once labeled is a thing understood, or so it would seem.

At issue is whether in fact most growth in urban areas has accumulated in a haphazard, inefficient, and undesirable manner at the urban periphery. The ribbon of development hugging the radial transportation routes leading out of the city, the suburban housing developments laced together by streets and accessible to commercial and retail activities only by automobile, and building densities so low that mass transit becomes infeasible—all these factors reinforce the notion that ongoing low-density development is leading to future urban forms that are wasteful of time, energy, and land resources. However, a case can be made that conventional wisdom may not be an entirely reliable guide to policy in this regard.

A common assumption among policymakers is that dispersion and the consequent development patterns at the periphery are somehow highly undesirable trends that need to be countered, if not reversed. In their place, policymakers call for efforts that channel growth into more historically familiar centralized and concentrated patterns. In addition, the concern surrounding America's energy dependence in recent years has reinforced the idea that dispersion and low-density living are bad and that concentration is good. However, indications are that there are multiple options for accommodating higher energy costs that make the prospect of a large-scale return to compact, centralized, high-density urban development extremely unlikely, if not actually detrimental. Firms and households will likely be able to avoid profligate energy consumption in a variety of ways without resorting to relocation. Actually, dispersion and low-density development may well offer several unappreciated advantages and opportunities in a resource-sensitive future. The guarded optimism offered by this reappraisal comes at an opportune time, because the long-term trend apparently is toward deconcentration and dispersal from traditional central city and older suburban locations.

Low-density development has generally been thought to squander energy and environmental resources and to engender mushrooming fiscal costs (both capital and operating) associated with extending public service infrastructures into low-density areas at the urban periphery. Yet, as cities get larger and more densely settled, the same factors that operate to make them more productive may also make them more costly to maintain and replace in terms of environment, energy, and fiscal resources.

An examination of low-density living might question the validity of these indictments. For instance, whether or not those who move to the suburbs continue to make high demands for community services, some analyses show that residents of high-density areas appear to require (and demand) more expensive packages of community services than those who live at low densities. If public service packages are viewed as so vitally important, why do households and firms continue to move where the service packages contain less than what these users previously enjoyed? For half a century, households and firms have been spatially sorting themselves, either purposefully or inadvertently, so that they have less and fewer of the traditional municipal services. This fact illustrates the willingness of households to internalize service costs by obtaining them privately or by consuming fewer or less of them from the public sector. Together with lower overall costs associated with suburban locations, a powerful incentive for low-density living exists: to relocate to locations where one can consume publicly those services or circumstances that one needs or desires, and can avoid supporting via taxes those services and circumstances that only others need.

A far-flung web of urban interdependence at lower densities has resulted in a large number of efficient and desirable consequences that are too easily overlooked or discounted. Because both jobs and people have left the central city, those who live in suburbs are increasingly able to work in them as well. This situation may allow a reduction in commuting between workplace and homeplace, with consequent time and energy cost savings. The dispersal of employment, residences, and commercial establishments lessens traffic congestion, air and noise pollution, and the demands placed on the streets, bridges, and infrastructure control systems (for example, traffic lights, street lighting systems) that convey and regulate job commuting and goods shipment into and out of central areas.

The energy gluttony associated with low density also may be overstated. Although residential heating and cooling systems and travel within the community account for most urban energy consumption, other factors condition the energy requirements of these activities. When computing consumption, the size of the average unit that must be heated and cooled clearly is as important as the density of buildings. Behemoth structures so often found in dense urban centers are associated with tremendous energy expenditures.

With regard to travel, accessibility is determined by many factors besides physical distance. Surely congestion and other factors impeding traffic flow make intra-city energy (and time) costs increasingly comparable to those in low-density areas. In addition, heavily concentrated population groupings separated by substantial distances create high interregional transportation costs for supplying goods; these may exceed the aggregate costs across lower density settlements involving shorter shipping distances.

With such qualifications, much of the energy consumption savings associated with high-density urban development patterns is wiped out. "In short, the savings in *total* urban energy consumption attributable to the shift from low-density residential sprawl to planned high density is about 3 percent and that attributable to the density factor alone is about 1 percent."[2] High-density growth and development, therefore, may not necessarily be more economically desirable than low-density growth and development.

With regard to air pollution, the harmful effects are a function of human exposure to substances at certain concentrations over periods of time, and not of total emissions per capita. As a rule, pollution exposure per capita is reduced in low-density settings. Even though dispersed settlement patterns may increase reliance on technologies that generate large amounts of pollutants, the per capita exposure to those pollutants is likely to be reduced. In addition, cleansing systems that use the natural flow of air and water are available to low-density urban areas, but are less useful for high-density settlements.

The capital cost savings attributable to construction in high-density areas are largely based on differences in dwelling unit square footage. Again, density of development *per se* masks a number of other factors that are principally responsible for the cost differences associated with high- and low-density development. Reason exists to believe that where energy and financial resources are scarce, lower density development patterns so often found at the urban periphery can offer the full range of savings available to traditionally higher density urban core areas. Not only may higher densities lead to accelerated deterioration of the urban physical forms, but also certain construction and maintenance projects (involving roads and sewer lines, for example) are immensely more expensive in high-density locations than in low-density areas.

With regard to the effects of patterns and density of land use on economic and fiscal costs, higher urban densities and larger metropolitan population sizes are associated with higher economic costs, including real estate prices, overall costs of living, private-sector wages, and local governmental operating costs. Although several of these indicators are more directly reflective of historical political and institutional legacies than of land use and density *per se,* urban policies crafted with explicit land-use objectives in mind should be considered carefully. Any marginal energy or cost savings gained by concentrated, mixed, land-use patterns might be quickly eclipsed by the tendency for explicit public policy to inflate the prices both of acquiring centrally located land and of operating and servicing the land uses.

Finally, what reply can be made to the assertion that encouraging low-density development sanctions the continued waste of existing central city public service infrastructures? The fiscal shortfall facing many beleaguered central cities often has been managed by deferring expenditures on required maintenance. However, even (if not especially) shrinking cities need to maintain their capability to deliver services to households and businesses. Yet, many aspects of the infrastructure are probably being rendered redundant as the contraction process continues, and carefully selected disinvestment of some services may be needed in an overall adjustment process. Furthermore, low-density growth and dispersal generally cannot be challenged purely on the grounds that it courts costly redundancy:

> [O]ne must distinguish between the myth and reality of central city infrastructures. We may decry what appears to be the expensive duplication in growth areas of the same facilities languishing in aging urban centers; however, we must realize that, in many cases, the older capital plants—sewer and water systems, for example—may be but remnants of a once glorious past, so long neglected that their

rehabilitation may be far more costly than start-
ing over again elsewhere.[3]

The evolving social and economic landscape at the
periphery of our older central cities may exhibit far more
order and efficiency than previously thought. A new form
of urban spatial organization is emerging. A technologically obsolete central city physical form that has traditionally performed innumerable functions for urban society is receding in favor of an urban landscape with multiple
dispersed centers of concentration and specialization. The
old central city is shedding its former functions as a center
of production and as a residence for a widely diverse urban
population and is evolving into a more narrowly specialized central business district. Many of the divested functions have been assumed by the newer commercial,
employment, and residential inner and outer suburbs,
often far removed from the central urban core. A new
hierarchy of places is emerging to accommodate simultaneously both decentralization and a dispersed reconcentration. Urban policy that is inconsistent with these larger
trends should be critically reexamined. Policy focused on
efforts to protect and to replace outmoded physical structures in evolving urban areas deserves special scrutiny, and
the implications of high- versus low-density development
should be carefully assessed.

During the next decade, a larger policy issue must be
squarely faced: What should be the role of the federal
government concerning the redistribution trends within
and among metropolitan areas and regions of the nation?
Although the rate of change no doubt will fluctuate to
some extent, the general direction of the trend is not likely
to alter during the rest of this century. Whether the revitalization of older cities should take precedence over further
growth in the suburbs and beyond deserves more careful
consideration. In short, should the federal government
pursue explicit urban policies that attempt to retard the
trends toward low-density growth and development, even
if they cannot be reversed?

Conventional arguments on this topic seldom emphasize the tradeoffs that simultaneously favor and disadvantage central cities and suburbs. Increasing economic
vitality of suburban areas and diminishing pressure on certain central city institutions, services, and facilities have
not been viewed as adequate compensation for increasing
congestion and tax burdens in suburban places and declining population and economic bases in central cities.
Indeed, policy efforts to retard or to reverse suburban
growth may court serious adverse consequences. For instance, any effort to slow the construction of new homes,

**Reconsidering
the Rebuilding
of the
Nation's Cities**

which are most often located in suburbs, would severely depress the housing construction industry (among the nation's largest) and its allied industries. It would reduce the range of housing types and location choices available for an increasing diversity of households and would probably drive up land prices, rents, and property taxes in central locations.

Another factor may also be too easily overlooked: The decentralization of population to the periphery has operated to improve the housing of Americans. Suburban growth has made a general upgrading possible for those who have left and for those who have been left behind. The majority population who have moved have benefitted from improvements in not only their housing, but also their job prospects, neighborhood and school quality, and quality of life in general. The resulting trickledown process, whereby increasingly better housing becomes available to the poor, has allowed a massive upgrading that may have been possible in no other way. For this reason, an urban policy designed to slow suburban growth may be neither desirable nor feasible.

Whether the middle class and industry abandon the cities to the poor or are constrained by public policy to remain, the poor ultimately suffer the most from the changes. The social, if not residential, segregation of the well-off may largely exacerbate the problem of being poor but does not cause it. To ameliorate the negative consequences arising from the transformation of the nation's communities, policy efforts should focus on helping the urban underclass of the poor and the dependent, and not on maintaining outdated urban structures and functions.

If anything, the dominant trend toward low-density development should be harnessed in such a way that those whose fortunes improve by moving out, regardless of their new locations, are not allowed to abandon their responsibilities to those who are left behind. Civic responsibilities should not be limited to place of residence. Public actions should assist those who have been left behind to adjust to the consequences of the departure of others. In that way, the multiple benefits and focused costs of suburban growth can be shared by all, wherever they live.

What can be said to those who view suburbanization as a process that is enervating our central cities by draining fiscal and other resources? Although federal policies for many years have marginally aided the dispersion process if only by speeding it up, public policy *per se* is unlikely to have sufficient influence to blunt the dominant trend toward deconcentration and dispersal. Reduced populations and low-density land uses may also translate into reduced intensity of demands on the deteriorating infrastructures and environmental amenities of our central cities.

The role and scope of central cities are changing. The central city is transforming to prepare it to play a new vital role in future urban life. Policy should not be devised to attempt a restoration of the central city's historic role in urban society, complete with a full array of functions that reflect an earlier technological and social era. The central city has ceased to do some things as well as other places; it will, however, continue to do other things exceedingly well. Policy should work with the dominant trends to ensure that the competitive strengths of the city are nurtured, not compromised or diluted by shoring up an outdated concept of the city.

Our cities will remain strong in the future; they will continue to be great generators of health, wealth, and welfare for the larger society. As such, they will continue to be true national assets. Their benefits will continue to accrue to both their residents and those who live well beyond their borders. They will be joined increasingly by noncentral and nonadjacent urban concentrations, and the full range of functions will be shared through a new urban division of labor. The city is the crucible of change in regional and national urban society. At all times, it must reflect the changing conditions and opportunities of social, political, economic, and cultural life.

Surely the older central cities as well as the newer ones should be viewed as national treasures, the responsibilities of all citizens. Local civic allegiances should be expanded into national civic allegiances. The fate of all people in all places is the responsibility of us all. National settlement patterns have become diverse; our common life depends on it, and our collective sentiments captured and implemented by public policies should foster the merging arrangements, not deny them. Urban policy should assist cities in all regions and of all sizes and ages to cope with and adjust to continued suburbanization; more households and firms will benefit from accommodating, rather than reversing, these trends.

1. J. D. Kasarda, "The Implications of Contemporary Redistribution Trends for National Urban Policy," paper contributed to the President's Commission for a National Agenda for the Eighties, Washington, D.C.: 1980, pp. 23-25. (Forthcoming in *Social Science Quarterly,* December 1980.)
2. A. Altshuler, "Review of the Costs of Urban Sprawl," *Journal of the American Institute of Planners,* Vol. 43 (April 1977):209. (Emphasis supplied.)
3. G. Sternlieb and J. W. Hughes, "The New Economic Geography of America," in *Revitalizing the Northeast: Prelude to an Agenda,* eds., G. Sternlieb and J. W. Hughes (New Brunswick, N.J.: Center for Urban Policy Research, 1978), p. 125.

Academy for Contemporary Problems. "Regional Patterns of Urban Growth and Decline in the United States." Washington, D.C.: U.S. Department of Housing and Urban Development, undated.

Alaman, P. and Birch, D. "Components of Employment Change for States, by Industry Group, 1970-1972." Cambridge: Joint Study for Urban Studies of MIT and Harvard University, 1975, working paper.

Altshuler, A. "Review of the Costs of Urban Sprawl," *Journal of the American Institute of Planners.* Vol. 43 (April 1977):207-209.

Bearse, P. "Toward a National Urban Policy—Critical Reviews, Influencing Capital Flows for Urban Economic Development: Incentives or Institution Building?" *Journal of Regional Science.* Vol. 19, No. 1 (1979):79-91.

Berry, B. J. L. and Silverman, L. P., eds. *Population Redistribution and Public Policy.* Washington, D.C.: National Academy of Sciences, 1980.

Downs, A. "Key Issues Concerning the Long-Range Policies and Programs of the U.S. Department of Housing and Urban Development." Washington, D.C.: Office of Policy Development and Research, U.S. Department of Housing and Urban Development, 1977.

Fuguitt, G. V., Voss, P. R., and Doherty, J. C. *Growth and Change in Rural America.* Washington, D.C.: The Urban Land Institute, 1979.

Glickman, N. J. "International Trade, Capital Mobility, and Economic Growth: Some Implications for American Cities and Regions in the 1980s," paper contributed to the President's Commission for a National Agenda for the Eighties, Washington, D.C., 1980.

Goodman, J. L., Jr. "Back to the City: Misperceptions of the '70s, Prospects for the '80s." Washington, D.C.: The Urban Institute, 1980, working paper.

Howell, J. M. "Urban Revitalization and Industrial Policy," testimony before the Subcommittee on the City, Committee on Banking, Finance, and Urban Affairs, U.S. House of Representatives, Washington, D.C., 1980.

Kasarda, J. D. "The Implications of Contemporary Redistribution Trends for National Urban Policy," paper contributed to the President's Commission for a National Agenda for the Eighties, Washington, D.C. and forthcoming in *Social Science Quarterly,* December 1980.

Kotler, M. and Sumka, H. J. "Is Residential Displacement a Critical Urban Problem?" *Urban Concerns Magazine* (February/March 1980):31-40.

Long, L. H. and De Are, D. "Migration to Nonmetropolitan Areas: Appraising the Trend and Reasons for Moving." Washington, D.C.: Bureau of the Census, U.S. Department of Commerce, 1979, draft report.

Parker, M. H. "Future and Continuing Problems and Opportunities in Nonmetropolitan America: The Prospect for the 1980s," paper contributed to the President's Commission for a National Agenda for the Eighties, Washington, D.C., 1980.

Rees, J. "Economic Development Trends in Non-Metropolitan and Suburban Communities." Washington, D.C.: President's National Urban Policy Report, U.S. Department of Housing and Urban Development, 1980, working paper.

Rees, J. and Bradley, R. "Changes in Economic Structure and Regional Decentralization Processes in the United States: The Policy Implications," paper contributed to the President's Commission for a National Agenda for the Eighties, Washington, D.C., 1980.

Schwartz, B. *The Changing Face of the Suburbs.* Chicago: University of Chicago Press, 1976.

Subcommittee on the City, Committee on Banking, Finance, and Urban Affairs, U.S. House of Representatives, 95th Congress, First Session. *Toward a National Urban Policy.* Washington, D.C.: U.S. Government Printing Office, 1977.

Subcommittee on the City, Committee on Banking, Finance, and Urban Affairs, U.S. House of Representatives, 96th Congress, Second Session. "Compact Cities: Energy Saving Strategies for the Eighties." Washington, D.C., forthcoming.

Sumka, H. J. "Neighborhood Revitalization and Displacement: A Review of the Evidence," *APA Journal* (October 1979):480-487.

U.S. Department of Housing and Urban Development. "Effects of Metropolitan Development Patterns: A Summary Report." Washington, D.C.: Office of Policy Development and Research, February 1, 1980, draft report.

U.S. Department of Housing and Urban Development. *The President's National Urban Policy Report.* Washington, D.C.: U.S. Government Printing Office, 1978.

U.S. Department of Housing and Urban Development. *The President's National Urban Policy Report.* Washington, D.C.: U.S. Government Printing Office, 1980.

U.S. Department of Transportation. *Transportation Agenda for the 1980s: Issues and Policy Directions.* Washington, D.C.: U.S. Government Printing Office, 1980.

Vining, D. R., Jr. Pallone, R. L., and Yang, C. H. "Population Dispersal from Core Regions: A Description and Tentative Explanation of the Patterns in 20 Countries." Philadelphia: University of Pennsylvania, 1980, working paper.

Wardwell, J. M. and Gilchrist, C. J. "Employment Deconcentration in the Nonmetropolitan Migration Turnaround." Draft article forthcoming in *Demography* 17 (May 1980).

Chapter 4

Local
ECONOMIC AND FISCAL
Distress

A s a result of national deconcentration trends, cities have lost much of their competitive edge over other locations as centers of production and residence. Although central locations and compact arrangements are, and will continue to be, economic and social assets for a wide variety of activities, they have gradually become obsolete and inefficient for other activities. As a consequence, selected households and firms—and their resources and allegiances—have migrated out of older central cities in great numbers. Similar patterns have emerged in many older suburbs, large metropolitan areas, and multistate regions.

Industrial disinvestment and residential outmigration have resulted in economic and fiscal consequences for beleaguered local governments and the increasingly dependent populations left behind. This chapter highlights those consequences and offers alternative options for managing them.

The shifting intrametropolitan, interregional, and transnational investment patterns of private industry often demonstrate remarkably little allegiance to political jurisdictions. Despite the necessity to encourage and enforce a measure of corporate social responsibility by firms, they must remain sufficiently unfettered to allow them to achieve as much productivity and to retain as much flexibility as possible for responding to shifting national and international economic crosscurrents. Our national economic vitality depends on them. Accordingly, firms must be reasonably free to invest, disinvest, and reinvest in a manner that gives them maximum ability to function and to thrive.

Industrial disinvestment tied to shifts of capital is manifested in several ways. Although the popular image (and visible symbol) is of a manufacturing plant closing in one location and reopening in another, this circumstance is quite rare. The actual physical relocation of a plant represents only about 2 percent of all private sector

Economic Distress: Industrial Disinvestment

employment change. More common forms of disinvestment are more subtle. Firms can disinvest from a location by delaying the maintenance of physical assets or by refusing to replace them as they are depleted. Firms with multiple plants may systematically shift personnel and/or equipment resources from one plant to another, effectively reducing the investment in one or more plants. Finally, firms may disinvest without relocating anything. Instead, the profits from one operation may be invested in alternative locations and operations.

All disinvestment strategies tend to disadvantage the localities to which a plant is anchored by creating a slowdown in employment growth. By shifting capital, firms can adjust to changing circumstances more rapidly than the people and localities depending on them directly for jobs and tax-base support. For those communities experiencing a contraction of their economic base as a result of industrial disinvestment, economic distress and fiscal distress threaten to become mutually reinforcing.

The emerging interregional disinvestment pattern has favored the West and later the South at the expense of the Northeast and Midwest. Between 1960 and 1976, the capital stock in the South grew twice as fast as that in the Northeast. Between 1966 and 1979, the industrial Northeast and Midwest lost nearly 800,000 manufacturing jobs, while national expansion added 2.3 million total jobs elsewhere. For every 100 manufacturing jobs created by new plants in the North, 111 were lost to some form of disinvestment. In the South, 80 manufacturing jobs were lost for every 100 added through new capital investment.

Although the South has benefitted from interregional economic shifts in the postwar decades, its advantages have the tendency to slip away at an even faster rate than they have from the Northeast and Midwest. For example, between 1969 and 1976, the South was the most likely region to experience the closing of a large manufacturing plant. In addition, industrial activity that was attracted to the South since the 1950s by lower wages, greater labor control, and lower energy costs now is often found relocating outside the United States to achieve even lower production costs.

As industrial activity becomes increasingly freed from specific locations in postindustrial America, economic gains of increased productivity and efficiency are secured by capital shifts and are registered in new locations. Such disinvestment patterns are accompanied by a residue of social costs that are anchored to the places, and experienced by the people, left behind. As this pattern moves across national borders, losses also are suffered by the

Federal Urban Policy Response to Economic Distress

national economy. Both movement patterns have invited urban policy responses.

The ongoing processes of shifting investment are generally viewed from the perspective of local and regional economic growth and development, rather than from the perspective of the overall national economy. This viewpoint is understandable given the predictable tendency for government to use public policies primarily to reconcile intrametropolitan and interregional conflicts.

It is reasonable for localities to do all that they can to strengthen and diversify their economic bases, and to expect that the federal government will at least not hinder their efforts. Nonetheless, both national and subnational urban policies have stressed reorienting what is perceived to be a perverse incentive system wired into public policies, because these incentives and policies are considered to be responsible for the private sector investment decisions that lead to the flow of capital and economic opportunity out of certain localities, regions, and even the nation itself.

Another equally predictable federal urban policy response to the locational consequences of private sector disinvestment is an attempt to redirect growth back to central cities by emphasizing reinvestment and incentive strategies as inducements. Business incentive policies, including tax credits and writedowns, loans, guarantees, subsidies (and even conditioning plant closures and relocations with an "exit" notice) are assumed to influence the cost-sensitive locational behavior of firms if they are large enough. Ironically, the widespread belief in the potency of incentives not only is unsubstantiated by empirical evidence, but also reflects a relatively primitive view of the private sector held by the public sector.

Economic development policies seldom appreciate that private sector relocation decisions often are more responsive to the noneconomic business climate than to vacillating cost differentials. The term "business climate" often suggests the absence of constraints and restrictions, rather than the presence of anything specific. Thus, an overly narrow concept of economic development that assigns primacy to capital and investment (and incentives believed to influence them) without greater sensitivity to ostensibly noneconomic factors influencing disinvestment and relocation should be critically reassessed.

Fiscal Distress: Balancing Resources and Responsibilities

Fiscal distress is an inevitable accompaniment of rapid fluctuation in population and employment levels that rise and fall out of step with one another. Between the 1880s and the Depression, when our nation's older cities experienced unprecedented growth, most cities were in dire fiscal straits because they had to finance expanded physical plants and service infrastructures. In the late 1970s, the threatened bankruptcy of older cities such as Cleveland and New York City often diverted attention to their political histories and cultures (not to mention bookkeeping legerdemain) to explain their financial problems. Such an approach, however, treats the phenomenon of fiscal distress as if it were episodic and isolatable and obscures its underlying dynamics. Local fiscal distress is best viewed as a systemic condition wherein local governments have more or less difficulty in reconciling shifts in their historical urban service functions with their revenue-generating capacities.

Local fiscal distress is conditioned by the fact that cities are the creatures of states. Their powers are limited to those explicitly granted by states. Furthermore, municipal revenue sources and expenditures are largely controlled by state law. The traditional and principal source of revenue granted to localities has been the property tax. Recently, however, local dependence on the property tax has lessened, particularly with regard to more specialized, nonschool urban services. Additionally, local property tax bases are shrinking as households, industry, and their taxable incomes migrate to other areas. Increasingly, localities respond to these two trends, which are aggravated by the erosion of purchasing power through inflation, by increasing their dependence on outside revenue sources. For example, nearly 40 percent of the revenues of the nation's older cities now comes from sources other than local taxes and user charges.

Primary reliance on the traditional property tax for revenues results in another fiscal problem—a lack of flexibility. Property taxes are generally less able to keep up with inflation-generated increases in municipal expenditures than income and sales taxes. Thus, during inflationary times, the most responsive revenue-generating tools (income and sales taxes) are those that state governments have reserved for themselves.

The occurrence of urban fiscal distress varies according to several characteristics of localities, such as size, region, and lifestage. Although fiscal distress is more common in older industrial regions such as the Northeast and the upper Midwest, large cities are more likely to display symptoms of fiscal distress than are small cities. However, a city's size is often less important than its age. Old cities are constrained by a number of historical economic and political legacies, including an inability to expand their borders through annexation to capture the outmigration of economic vitality, and a responsibility for a relatively elaborate service package for their residents.

Although older industrial cities are more likely to experience fiscal distress, this problem is not an inevitable

44

consequence of achieving a particular lifestage. Older cities' fiscal distress also may be related to large maintenance costs for their public service infrastructures. Younger cities, on the other hand, often face fiscal distress because of a lack of institutional capacity to meet the needs of a quickly expanding population, requiring substantial physical construction and service facility expansion expenditures. In short, cities in all regions, of all sizes and ages, are experiencing increasing difficulty in matching resources with responsibilities.

The constellation of factors that predispose a locality to fiscal distress are many and varied. Beyond those related to the economic and demographic trends, several other factors deserve mention. Local governments are unequally susceptible to inflationary pressures because labor costs constitute a significant proportion of local expenditures. The differential, and often heightened, impact of cyclical economic declines on cities reduces their tax receipts while increasing the demand for services. Finally, the mix of revenue sources available to a locality may both hamper its ability to cope with inflationary pressures and reduce its flexibility in putting together a tax package that can maximize revenue generation but minimize the burden on the poor and the dependent.

Because urban fiscal distress is related to an imbalance between provided services and available revenues, a search for policy options to remedy this imbalance should involve an examination of: (1) the character of the service package and the level of expenditures, and (2) the composition of revenue sources. This omits, for the time being, the larger contextual macroeconomic policies that may be needed to stimulate economic growth and retard inflation.

Managing Local Fiscal Distress: Adjusting Urban Service Packages

Just as there is no inherently overdeveloped public sector, there is no limit on citizens' demands for services or on the political process' capability to translate those demands into service packages. Population and economic-base expansion leads not only to dependable revenue expansion, but also to the public provision of a wide variety of local services. Problems develop when growth cannot be maintained or when growth rates vary among these factors.

The package of urban services offered by some jurisdictions has become too elaborate to be maintained into the future. Service trimming therefore is often suggested as a means of reflecting the shrinkage of the tax and population bases. However, political constraints have traditionally militated against lowering service levels or dropping certain services altogether. Not only recipients bemoan these adjustments, but also service providers feel threatened by service package trimming. Well entrenched public employee unions and constituent subgroups of citizens who depend on specific services make public sector cutbacks to achieve the desired fiscal balance exceedingly difficult. Numerous localities have had to make difficult and painful choices before cutting back public services to reduce their service burdens. Pittsburgh, Baltimore, and Wilmington, Del., are examples of localities that have had some success in reducing public service expenditures.

Ironically, the utility of this option is diminished by the fact that service "needs," as they have come to be defined, do not show the same capacity to shrink as tax bases. In fact, given the selectivity of the households and industries left behind, the range, density, and severity of needs requiring a governmental response may expand as the available resources to fund those responses contract.

Another means of reducing service package costs is by delaying maintenance of the service infrastructure. However, such expenditure reductions may be illusory at best. Neglect of infrastructure not only may entail increased repair costs in the future, but also may quicken the pace of outmigration by households and firms.

The more common policy options, however, assume achieving fiscal balance by replacing revenue loss and maintaining traditional service packages. This strategy not only is more politically palatable, but also recognizes that cities perform areawide, regional, and even national functions for urban America. The needs of the people residing in these cities, if not those of local governments, may be viewed as the result of being left behind by the outmigration of others. If the actions of those who move outside the nation's cities so dictate what happens to those who live inside those cities, then the ensuing responsibilities become state and national, not simply local.

Local Policy Options for Replacing Revenue Loss

In spite of the diversity of state-local relationships, the commonality of economic and demographic shifts that communities have to cope with leads to a limited array of fiscal options to recapture revenue loss while retaining service levels: (1) increasing the existing tax rates, (2) shifting or adding tax burdens to new tax bases, (3) substituting service user charges for taxes, (4) shifting the source of services from the public to the private sector (privatization), and (5) shifting service provision and financing responsibilities to another level of government. To this inventory might be added the adoption of improved financial accounting methods. Financial reporting procedures vary tremendously among cities, and the need for improvement is acute. However, cities do not experience revenue loss because of bad bookkeeping, and a "management fix" rarely will be sufficient to avoid the problem.

Increasing existing tax rates is clearly an option. However, this approach has been at least partly responsible for the outmigration of economic activity and for the decline in the revenue-generating capacity of local jurisdictions. Shifting to new mixes of tax sources may help to redistribute the tax burden from one group to another within the city, but this option may be self-defeating, because those most able to pay may be those most willing and able to relocate to avoid an increased tax burden. The political gains realized through local redistribution of tax burdens may do little to increase the revenue prospects of a locality. Both of these fiscal options work to reinforce the deconcentration trends that fuel fiscal distress, and therefore are self-defeating.

Financing public services through user charges (fee for service) has grown in popularity. The adoption of this mechanism is possible because many services provided by the public sector have an essentially private character (libraries, parks, museums, recreation facilities). Thus, prices may be charged on the basis of benefits received. User charges promote equity by assuring that citizens pay a price proportionate to the quantity of the service consumed. Efficiency is promoted because user charges provide demand signals concerning which services, and how much of each, the citizenry wants. Given the limited capabilities of municipalities to provide services, user charges help to ensure that a service will be provided for and received by those who value it the most, assuming that they can pay the fee. An added advantage is that user charges are linked to the actual consumption of a service, not to the eligibility for consumption that is tied to residence. Thus, services are paid for by those who use them, regardless of their residence status in the jurisdiction. This strategy may exclude the urban poor from receiving a service if they cannot afford it, but the traditional regressive local property tax systems often force the poor to subsidize through general taxation unwanted services enjoyed largely by others.

The private provision of traditionally public services is also increasingly used as a fiscal option, particularly by relatively young and growing jurisdictions. Prospective cost savings is generally not the reason for using this option; private service provision is not necessarily more efficient than public service provision. Instead, a city's growing inability to meet demands is often the impetus for contracting arrangements. Privatization also is particularly attractive to communities that seek to avoid substantial fiscal outlays required to establish a service infrastructure that accommodates recent growth or that meets episodic or seasonal needs. However, the use of contracting and service agreements by local governments is better suited for newly added services and those whose production, delivery, and consumption entail a minimum of uncertainty.

Although not a fiscal option, another method of relieving fiscal distress is available to localities. They should be encouraged to give careful attention to the reality and the image of their business climate. By projecting an attractive business climate (albeit subjective and amorphous), they can increasingly compete for primary investment and secondary expansion under certain conditions.

Although the fiscal options available to local governments are limited and sometimes self-defeating, other governmental bodies can provide assistance. Revenue-generation strategies at the metropolitan, state, and federal government levels can help to ease (if not eliminate) local fiscal distress.

Nonlocal Policy Options for Replacing Local Revenue Loss

Given the tendency for localities to lose tax bases through the outmigration of households and industry, the use of metropolitan-scale strategies to capture revenue loss is attractive, despite the political obstacles that prevent their more frequent adoption. Tax-base sharing, annexation, city-county consolidation, and other metropolitan reform strategies can help to distribute more uniformly the economic growth that exists outside central cities and to provide an expanded tax base for financing public services. In addition, federal and state assistance may be usefully allocated to metropolitan areas rather than to traditional political jurisdictions (cities, counties) within them. However, where and under what conditions metropolitan areas become principal recipients of state and/or federal aid demands careful examination.

These strategies attempt to expand effective, if not actual, political boundaries so that they coincide with the expanded social and economic scale of the metropolitan area. The growth equalization of revenues across all jurisdictions within the metropolitan area may help to lessen disparities among service packages received by citizens in different jurisdictions. Lessening disparities among jurisdictions also may help to stem the relocation of households or firms from a central to a peripheral location within a metropolitan area by alleviating the incentive of reduced tax burdens. However, because need is not distributed uniformly across a metropolitan area, this strategy may provide service "output" equality, but not service "outcome" equality. Inequalities in service distribution arrangements can be justified as a compensatory strategy to ameliorate the existing unequal distribution of needs and the unequal ability to meet needs privately across population subgroups.

The role of state governments in responding to the fiscal dilemmas of their cities is quite properly receiving

48

increased attention. Since a city and its powers are defined by the state, some problems faced by a city can rightly be laid at the doorstep of state governments. Although federal fiscal relief to localities has increased dramatically through most of the 1970s, unrestricted state aid has not increased significantly since the 1950s. For that reason, suggested remedies include greater direct state aid through direct cash grants or operating subsidies, or by granting cities the right to adopt other revenue-generating tools (such as city sales or income taxes).

Although widespread state budget surpluses may be viewed as justification for increased state aid to localities, those surpluses may only be temporary. A more valid reason for advocating increased state assumption of responsibility for their localities' fates is that many state governments have increased significantly their managerial capacities to assist localities in the past two decades.

Local fiscal health may also be promoted by the transfer to state government of the fiscal and/or administrative responsibility for selected local services. Two candidates for transfer include elementary and secondary education and public welfare, unless or until the latter is nationalized. However, fiscal relief resulting from these transfers may not be substantial. Welfare already is a state function in most jurisdictions, and state assumption of education expenditures would probably result in offsetting local taxes by state taxes. Although the overall tax burden on local residents would not be lessened, potential local revenues could be shifted to other expenditure areas. The loss of local control over traditionally local functions is one example of the potentially undesirable outcomes that attend increasing local fiscal dependence on state resources.

Another increasingly recommended strategy is state property tax circuit-breaker programs. These are designed to limit property tax payments of low-income households to a fixed percentage of their income and to subsidize the shortfall with cash rebates or income tax credits. Most states have already adopted this mechanism for assisting low-income elderly citizens. This system stimulates a flow of state revenue that would clearly have spatial consequences, because central cities are the site of most large proportions of poor households.

Recently, the phenomenon of state fiscal containment initiatives (Proposition 13) has received a great deal of attention. In the past 5 years, nearly half of the states have adopted limitations on local taxes or on state revenues and expenditures. Whether containment takes the form of a local property tax rollback through cuts in the tax rate, the indexing of state income taxes to inflation, or "cap laws" restricting future growth in state or local expenditures, a variety of social costs go largely unrecognized. Political jurisdictions may be forced to increase their reliance on taxes that are relatively more regressive, and social services for the poor and the dependent will probably bear the brunt of the budget adjustments. Cuts in public sector workforces threaten to be deepest among youth, women, and minorities—those who have relied on job expansion in this sector, but who are not sufficiently protected by seniority to weather public sector contraction. Finally, as states and localities herald containment measures as a control for a runaway public sector and as a way to exercise local autonomy, they ironically increase the likelihood of even greater dependence on federal government aid.

Federal policy options that propose remedying, if not reversing, local revenue loss also merit close attention. Federal options either may assist local fiscal efforts directly or may offer aid by refraining from actions that harm localities. These strategies can (but need not) be distinct. The federal government may directly subsidize the interest rates on locally issued taxable bonds, allowing localities to raise interest rates to attract more investor resources. The higher interest expenditures incurred by local governments as a result of increased investor resources could be partially assumed by the federal government.

In contrast, tax exemptions and concessions offered by state and local governments as incentives to lure industry into an area not only have often been ineffectual in increasing employment and output, but also entail the cost of forgone and sorely needed tax revenues. Punitive federal action, such as withholding federal grant funds, could be reserved for jurisdictions using tax exemptions as industrial location incentives.

The transfer of selected services from subnational government levels to the federal level also would help to relieve the fiscal distress experienced by local jurisdictions. The beneficial effects might be direct, involving the transfer of a local function to the federal government, or indirect, as when a state function is assumed by the federal government, freeing state revenues for potential local uses.

Four sets of federal actions directly influence local fiscal opportunities: (1) federal grant programs; (2) federal tax expenditures; (3) federal actions affecting local fiscal responsibilities; and (4) federal actions that impose expenditure obligations. Federal intergovernmental aid to cities has been important in reducing local fiscal distress where it has been identified and in delaying it where it has been threatening. Between 1972 and 1977, federal intergovernmental aid helped stabilize local tax burdens. On a per capita basis, state and local outlays increased by 131 percent between 1970 and 1978. By contrast, federal aid to states and localities went up by 218 percent, while federal aid for cities increased from $1.3 billion in 1970 to $8.9 billion in 1977.

Local governments have become increasingly dependent on federal intergovernmental aid, but these funds come with many strings attached. Local government costs associated with federal mandates have been substantial. Federal actions often place requirements on localities either to undertake new responsibilities engendering new costs or to cease activities that have a potential to raise revenues. An examination of the local fiscal impacts of several federal programs shows that the per capita burden shifted to local governments often exceeds the amount received in general revenue sharing funds. In addition, some programs originally funded by federal funds lock localities into continuing commitments long after the federal monies have been discontinued.

Alaman, P. and Birch, D. "Components of Employment Change for States, by Industry Group, 1970-1972." Cambridge: Joint Study for Urban Studies of MIT and Harvard University, 1975, working paper.

Bunce, H. L. and Goldberg, R. L. *City Need and Community Development Funding.* Office of Policy Development and Research, U.S. Department of Housing and Urban Development. Washington, D.C.: U.S. Government Printing Office, 1979.

Chinitz, B., ed. *Central City Economic Development.* Cambridge: Abt Books, 1979.

Claggett, W. "The Public-Private Connection in Urban Policy: Selected Aspects of Intersector Partnerships to Achieve Balanced National Growth and Economic Revitalization," report contributed to the President's Commission for a National Agenda for the Eighties, Washington, D.C., 1980.

Colman, W. G. *Cities, Suburbs, and States: Governing and Financing Urban America.* New York: Macmillan Publishing Co., Inc., 1975.

Dommel, P. R., Nathan, R. P., Liebschutz, S. F., Wrightson, M.T., and Associates, The Brookings Institution. *Decentralizing Community Development.* U.S. Department of Housing and Urban Development. Washington, D.C.: U.S. Government Printing Office, 1978.

Fisk, D., Kiesling, H., and Muller, T. *Private Provision of Public Services: An Overview.* Washington, D.C.: The Urban Institute, 1978.

Gorham, W. and Glazer, N., eds. *The Urban Predicament.* Washington, D.C.: The Urban Institute, 1976.

Norton, R. D. *City Life-Cycles and American Urban Policy.* New York: Academic Press, Inc., 1979.

Pascal, A. H. and Menchik, M. D. *Fiscal Containment: Who Gains? Who Loses?* Santa Monica: Rand Corporation, 1979.

Pascal, A. H., Menchik, M. D., Chaiken, J. M., Ellickson, P. L., Walker, W. E., De Tray, D. N., and Wise, A. E. *Fiscal Containment of Local and State Government.* Santa Monica: Rand Corporation, 1979.

Samuels, H. J. "Rationale for the Nation's Support of Small Business," paper contributed to the Small Business Conference for the White House, Washington, D.C., 1980.

Schwartz, G. G. *Bridges to the Future: Forces Impacting Urban Economies.* Columbus, Ohio: The Academy for Contemporary Problems, 1978.

Sternlieb, G. and Hughes, J. W., eds. *Post-Industrial America: Metropolitan Decline and Inter-Regional Job Shifts.* New Brunswick, N.J.: Center for Urban Policy Research, 1975.

Sternlieb, G. and Hughes, J. W., eds. *Revitalizing the Northeast: Prelude to an Agenda.* New Brunswick, N.J.: Center for Urban Policy Research, 1978.

U.S. Department of Housing and Urban Development. *The President's National Urban Policy Report.* Washington, D.C.: U.S. Government Printing Office, 1980.

Weinstein, B. L. and Clark, R. J. "Urban Trends and the Condition of Cities." Washington, D.C.: Southern Growth Policies Board, 1979, draft report.

Chapter 5

Social Distress
AND THE URBAN UNDERCLASS

> To recognize that irreversible changes in the eco-
> nomic environment have taken place is the first
> step toward taking responsibility for policies that
> perpetuate a dependent underclass. In the long
> run, [redevelopment] seems to offer little if any
> hope of restoring the upgrading process. Hence
> the outlook for the minority poor will improve
> only when their fate is cut loose from that of the
> declining cities. Of course, the reverse is also true.
> Perhaps the surest means of easing the transition
> for the industrial cities is to free them from the
> burden of the minority poor.[1]

I f the nation's settlements are allowed to transform
in accordance with the changing requirements of an
emerging 21st-century economy and society, the transitional costs cannot be ignored, even though they
may result in long-term benefits for the nation. The suffering of people caught in the evolution of larger urban economic systems is a day-to-day phenomenon and should not
be approached in the detached manner of an urban histor-
ian. An urban economy that is no longer confined to central
cities and that can no longer provide services for the dependent poor or jobs for unskilled or displaced workers shifts
the burden of change to those who are least able to bear it.
Efforts to help the urban underclass should not be limited by
underemphasizing or ignoring alternative policy responses
simply because they do not protect city-based political
power or restore cities to their former lofty positions.

Such social distress experienced by an urban underclass of the poor and the dependent who have been left
behind in the cities is the focus of this chapter. In addition
to the policy orientation problem outlined above, this section also discusses various methods of reducing social distress: assisting people who wish to relocate to places that
hold economic opportunities and retraining the displaced
worker and training the unskilled worker to enable them to
take part in the job market mainstream.

Cities are called on to display two disparate sets of characteristics. First, they must exhibit enough stability to meet the essential needs of their resident citizens and nonresident constituents. Far more Americans directly depend on cities daily than live in or even visit them. The emphasis is on continuity, being a predictable source of respite and relief, opportunity and order. At the same time, cities must be sufficiently flexible to adapt to the economic and demographic trends that constantly transform their relationships with their residents, neighboring localities, the region, the nation, and the world. The myriad responsibilities that they are assigned do not vary predictably with the resources that they have available. As levels of population and employment fluctuate in a community, one or more forms of urban distress often result.

Urban distress is a generic term that includes both institutional and individual aspects. Both forms of urban distress are not new, but given the traditional welfare functions of cities in urban societies, the distress afflicting urban institutions is relatively recent in origin. For the large older cities, institutional distress can be traced to the limited flexibility of historical political institutions and fiscal arrangements to adapt to fluctuating urban conditions and circumstances. Deteriorating physical structures and shortfalls in funding municipal services have become both cause and consequence of departing households and employment opportunities.

By contrast, the distress afflicting individuals is an age-old aspect of urban life. This social distress relates to the roles that cities have always performed for the larger society—to provide services, to acculturate newcomers, and to supply job opportunities for the unskilled or the inadequately skilled. Consequently, just as a hospital is the perennial setting for illness and attempts to treat it, cities have been the collection point for people in need of income, education, housing, health care, and employment.

A regional reality overlays this analysis. Social (individual) distress is more likely to be found in the South, while fiscal and economic (institutional) distress are more likely to be found in the Northeast. Whether socioeconomic conditions are measured by overall income levels, percentages of poverty, or per capita income, southern urban residents are poorer than urban residents in the rest of the country. That regional reality must be qualified, however, by recognizing that most indicators of social distress are not limited to specific regions, and that tremendous diversity exists within all regions. Assistance that keys squarely on regional targets may lose its capability to differentiate within regions and to direct aid to subregional locations and their residents.

54

In the past half-century, the least distressed households have been able to migrate to the suburbs and beyond, leaving behind an urban underclass—the poor and the powerless, the disadvantaged and the dependent. Ironically, conditions in cities may appear to have become worse largely because cities have performed their functions for society so well. Unlike hospitals, which measure their success by their capability to discharge patients whose health has been restored, the success of cities is evaluated by the circumstances of those left behind.

Our cities may never be rid of social distress, even though both individual and institutional distress may be the subject of meaningful amelioration. Although each can nourish the other, fiscal and economic distress do not necessarily accompany social distress. Where they coexist, independent policies may be required. Consequently, institutional remedies, such as strategies of metropolitan reorganization, aid to local governments and businesses, or even functional aid programs in manpower development, housing, transportation, or local economic development, may do little or nothing to assuage social distress.

Most current federal aid programs that are directed at ameliorating urban distress focus on problems more closely associated with intermediary institutions (including schools, workplaces, departments of local government or neighborhoods) than with individuals directly. One reason for this focus is the widely appreciated linkages between circumstances afflicting people and those afflicting places and institutions. Although such linkages exist, reliance on policy instruments that relieve institutional distress in order to relieve individual distress may overly simplify a bewildering and complex pattern of relationships.

Urban policy that is designed to remedy the problems facing people indirectly by remedying the problems facing local governments or businesses directly deserves some reanalysis. Policies aimed at remedying fiscal, economic, and/or physical structure distress may help remedy the ills of distressed cities without necessarily having much impact on the ills afflicting an urban underclass. In addition, such federal aid policies with an explicit urban focus are intended to alleviate poverty—a condition associated with life in cities, but not exclusively so.

Despite the importance of recognizing the general distress created by shifting local and regional economic bases, which have often resulted in imbalances between resources and responsibilities,

> . . . neutralizing the old city's fiscal legacy is only
> one step in an attack on the basic urban problem.
> That basic problem is viewed . . . not as one of city

Responding to Institutional Versus Individual Distress

governments, but rather of city residents, and in particular . . . the continuing concentration of the minority poor in cities offering diminishing job opportunities.[2]

Urban poverty, reflected in chronic unemployment, episodic displacement, or unemployability, is probably more directly the consequence of the lack of marketable skills, locational mismatches between jobs and people, and the problems of job access in structured labor markets than of deficiencies in other forms of capital. Although economic opportunity may exist in abundance, urban poverty persists in the midst of plenty because of the maldistribution of that opportunity or access barriers to it.

In large part, then, urban poverty requires an approach that emphasizes the potential for a redistribution of economic opportunity and/or the unemployed or underemployed who can work. Linking people to economic opportunity has never been accomplished exclusively within localities. Rather, it has often required that people relocate to settings where opportunities exist. Jobs-to-people urban strategies should be supplemented by more emphasis on people-to-jobs strategies and programs, which assist people willing to migrate to the location of new opportunities. Urban programs aimed solely at ameliorating poverty where it occurs may not help either the locality or the individual if the net result is to shackle distressed people to distressed places.

Urban programs may also provide direct assistance to those for whom the functioning of local, regional, and national labor markets is largely irrelevant. For the disproportionate number of the unskilled, minority youth, females heading households, elderly, and even some working poor who may temporarily or permanently comprise an urban underclass, assistance tied to job expansion or other community and economic development approaches may be largely ineffectual. For those who cannot work, aid independent of economic development strategies is required.

In the coming decade, many communities most certainly will experience a continuing inability to compensate fully for their loss of economic vitality, which is so often tied to the transformation of their economic bases. This situation will probably persist even though the bulk of out-migration of people and jobs, income and capital, is probably completed. In the not too distant future, an adjustment process could well unfold in some older large cities, accompanied by local revitalization at new, lower levels of population and employment. However, the massive losses of industrial employment probably will not be recouped, even during cyclical upswings in the nation's economy, and

Industrial Transformation and the Displaced Worker

56

the middle class probably will not return to the central city in large numbers. Chances are that this prediction will also be valid for newer cities, suburbs, and entire metropolitan areas.

Challenging the "myth of the return of manufacturing," the "forces leading to the decline of cities and regions are powerful and the federal government cannot reverse them," and so the nation must accept that "manufacturing is the past, not the future, of older central cities."[3] Instead, the economic function of cities is changing—from a center for production to one of service consumption. The inability of the service sector to compensate fully for manufacturing employment losses makes the picture even more stark. In addition, the compressed timeframes involved in the transformation process also hamper adaptation.

In the wake of this transformation, greater priority should be given to the displaced worker who bears the brunt of industrial restructuring and disinvestment. Future national, regional, and local economic planning should nurture the creation and adoption of new institutions to assist the displaced worker. Efforts should be made to train or retrain these workers to make them competitive in rapidly changing labor markets. For example, assisted mid-life retooling becomes increasingly more important because industries that workers enter in their youth can often lose their competitiveness while the worker is too young to retire or too laden with family responsibilities to incur alone the costs of new skills acquisition.

In addition, where possible and desirable, displaced workers should be assisted in migrating, if they so choose, to places offering more opportunities. A more equitable incomes policy also could be developed to reduce unjustified income inequality among people and regions. Additionally, workers in threatened industries could be encouraged and assisted in increasing their participation at the work site in order to improve worker productivity.

Improving Access to Economic Opportunity: Relocation and Retraining

A current major urban policy theme has stressed aiding people where they live by implementing various jobs-to-people strategies. Improvement in the condition of the urban poor principally has relied on narrowly defined urban economic development efforts to revitalize economically declining cities that have been traditionally dependent on manufacturing.

This general policy theme has been legitimized largely through the War on Poverty efforts and related place-oriented policy, such as urban renewal, the Model Cities program, the Community Action program, as well as more recent federal aid transfers to local governments and neighborhoods. However, such policy stands in contradistinction to the historical role of migration as the dominant means of linking people to opportunity.

"A common thread of all mass migrations in U.S. history has been the search for economic opportunity. . . . Migration is perhaps best defined as one form of human response to the uneven spatial distribution of opportunities and resources."[4] During the first half of this century, our nation's poor have migrated on a mass scale, particularly the rural poor moving into northern cities. The migration west and south of people seeking economic opportunity also has assumed major proportions.

Although aided over past decades immeasurably by technological advances, the mobility of Americans today is increasingly limited by a variety of social, legal, and institutional factors. States and suburban communities are voicing no-growth or restrictive growth sentiments that are often aimed at reducing environmental degradation. Minorities and households of certain compositions (single persons, single parent families) are often limited to selected residential areas because of the unavailability of appropriate housing, jobs, transportation, and special services (such as day care) and the more subtle barriers of sex, race, and lifestyle discrimination. Middle-class mobility and migration are hampered by tremendous financial and psychological investments in housing and community, and the difficulty of refinancing and relocating a household with two or more working members. The spatial segregation of the young, the old, the single, and the poor also increasingly translates into migration barriers for Americans. For these reasons, as well as "tilts" in contemporary urban policy that inadvertently anchor unemployed and displaced workers while attempts are made to import economic opportunity, short-distance mobility and long-distance migration are increasingly perceived as unattractive or irrelevant strategies for linking people with economic opportunity.

Urban policies today subtly reinforce the notion that an urban underclass is best helped "in place." Certainly, part of this conviction is based on the belief that big city bureaucracies can relatively efficiently identify the poor and distribute money and in-kind services to them. Administrative handling of problems is generally considered more efficient if the poor are concentrated within political jurisdictions. The fact that the poor and their multiple afflictions might also be aggravated through this concentration process has not always been fully appreciated. Although dispersing a problem may not solve it, a healthier environment may reduce the contagion effect, as illustrated by the urban ghetto, that militates against urban remedies.

Other, less charitable reasons exist for the lack of support for developing policies that assist people with problems to relocate from places with problems. The national perspective on local urban strategies is conditioned by a wide variety of social and political factors. Middle-class whites—and middle-class blacks—guard their social and physical separation from the urban underclass. An array of political forces (zoning restrictions, building codes) supports an approach that keeps the poor where they are. Furthermore, the nation's elected officials understandably prefer urban policies and aid strategies that are oriented toward places, because these tools allow them to enhance their resources in an urban system that continues to make more political, than social or economic, sense. Finally, the recent development of community opposition to growth of any sort to avoid environmental degradation and natural resource distress also is often a thinly veiled attempt to keep out the poor, especially the minority poor.

For these reasons, related to social exclusion, political base protection, and policy inertia, the United States has no program:

> . . . to help underemployed, unemployed, and low income persons in lagging areas to move and find employment in areas with greater opportunities. European experience . . . together with labor mobility demonstration projects in the United States, have shown that such programs are effective. . . . Failure to institute a permanent program of comprehensive relocation assistance is perhaps the most deficient aspect of . . . spatial resource allocation in the United States.[5]

The United States is virtually the only developed capitalist nation without policies or programs that assist the migration of people who are willing to follow employment opportunities. In Europe, mobility assistance programs are relatively well developed and enjoy considerable legitimacy. Presumably some portions of such people-to-jobs policy strategies could be imported.

The Organization for Economic Cooperation and Development has considered several relocation assistance strategies used in Europe:

- ☐ Establishment of a national employment information clearinghouse to facilitate interregional migrations among regional labor markets.
- ☐ Provision of travel assistance for workers who are relocating to start specific jobs.
- ☐ Provision of money to assist workers to commute during the early stages—after finding a job in another locality and before relocating their household.
- ☐ Provision of transitional assistance to ease the burden of relocation expenses while awaiting the first paycheck.

□ Maintenance of room and board facilities or subsidies for single workers, especially when they travel to obtain training required by a job.

□ Provision of youth hostels for relocated young workers.

□ Provision of separation and travel allowances for married workers who have found distant jobs and who need assistance to return home for visits instead of or prior to relocating the family.

□ Subsidization or complete coverage of moving costs.

□ Provision of housing search and resettlement assistance.

Reciprocal information networks among regions, industries, and segments of the labor force, as well as money and in-kind adjustment services, also appear to be crucial to the successful operation of a relocation program.

Many large public and private sector employers already provide these and many other relocation aids for their white-collar workers. Unfortunately, such transition and migration assistance packages are generally not available for unemployed or underemployed persons. Actions to aid the urban underclass therefore should focus on developing migration assistance for those who wish to participate. Although the expense may not be insignificant, this package of short-term aid could well serve as a substitution for relatively long-term welfare payments, which at best maintain, but seldom improve, the circumstances of the displaced worker.

The exportability of these strategies from the European experience to our own is a justifiable concern, especially considering the distribution pattern of the U.S. economy and the decentralization of our political structure. Fortunately, the results of a series of mobility demonstration projects conducted by the Department of Labor between 1965 and 1969 lend support for the viability of these kinds of labor relocation programs. Under their aegis, some 14,000 unemployed and underemployed workers were relocated with the assistance of relocation allowances. The results indicated that the vast majority were satisfied with their moves and that they probably would not have been able to relocate without the assistance.

Cash allowances are probably less important than noncash forms of assistance. Help in locating a home, arrangement of preemployment trips for interviews and training, family relocation counseling, and an extensive and responsive job clearing system to match workers with employment opportunities in regional and national job markets are particularly essential. Relating individual workers to appropriate labor markets reflects the likelihood that access to the relatively small-scale labor market within metropolitan areas (where the social and economic barriers between central city and suburb would have to be crossed) may be far more difficult than breaking into relatively similar labor markets between metropolitan areas or entire regions. In many instances, for an unemployed laborer in Buffalo to move into a job matching his qualifications in Phoenix may be more feasible than resolving a local mismatch between the location of jobs and the residence of workers.

The judicious combination of support services and relocation grants would be beneficial to workers and their families as they negotiate the extremely complex regional and national labor market systems. These strategies would also probably meet current popular demands for efficiency:

> [S]ociety benefits greatly from these relocation projects. . . . These pilot projects show that there is a sizeable group of unemployed workers who are willing to relocate to obtain employment. Providing relocation assistance to these people is the least expensive governmental method of providing employment for them. For those unwilling or unable to move, unemployment insurance and welfare payments will be available. What is important is giving the unemployed worker a choice, rather than condemning him to unemployment. . . .[6]

Robust federal efforts in manpower development and training were initiated nearly two decades ago. The Manpower Development and Training Act of 1962 established for the federal government a dominant role in the financing and administration of a variety of programs aimed at acquiring skills, developing employability, and providing jobs and work experience. The Comprehensive Employment and Training Act of 1973 significantly shifted the control of program funding to local governments, although the fiscal dependence of localities on the federal government was demonstrably increased in the process.

A large proportion of the urban underclass cannot be absorbed into the private sector economy because they lack skills demanded by modern society. Efforts should continue to train those who have never had marketable skills and to retrain those whose skills have been rendered obsolete or redundant. With the ultimate goal of securing private sector employment for these workers, supplemental and transitional public employment programs are justified so that all who can work are able to do so. Improved access to economic opportunity through relocation or retraining or both is less relevant for a sizeable portion of the urban underclass who cannot work and for those who work in low-wage sectors of the economy. As always this residual class can best be assisted through a more coherent blend of social policies and programs.

Any effort to revitalize the nation's economy necessarily requires an examination of local economic conditions and circumstances in relation to national and international economic and geopolitical trends. To some extent, although not entirely, the large-scale trends suggest that the articulation within a national economic system requires more than linking people and jobs within local or regional markets. Although workers may be permanently unemployed or underemployed in one region, opportunities that are (at best) illusory in their communities may exist in other near or distant places and may be realized by assisting in their relocation. Whereas so many economic development policies have been relatively ineffective in bringing jobs to people, in the very least a people-to-jobs emphasis derives potency from the fact that it works with, rather than against, larger economic and social trends.

In the light of the large-scale economic transformations under way, policies that hold the distressed place-distressed people linkage inviolate, and that try to improve the fortunes of both in each other's presence, may be misguided and misinformed. Public policy should seek to loosen the tie between distressed people and distressed places just as a variety of technological developments has loosened the ties between industry and its traditional urban location.

1. R. D. Norton, *City Life-Cycles and American Urban Policy* (New York: Academic Press, Inc., 1979), p. 171.
2. Ibid., p. 167.
3. D. E. Shalala, "Urban Is Our Middle Name: New Strategies for HUD," in *Central City Economic Development,* ed., B. Chinitz (Cambridge: Abt Books, 1979), p. 61.
4. B. L. Weinstein and J. Rees, "Sunbelt/Frostbelt Confrontation?" *Society* (May-June 1980): 19.
5. N. Hansen, *Location Preferences, Migration and Regional Growth* (New York: Praeger, 1973), pp. 62-63.
6. Ibid., p. 48.

Bradley, R. B. "The Continuing Significance of Race: An Inventory of Selected Trends," paper contributed to the President's Commission for a National Agenda for the Eighties, Washington, D.C., 1980.

Chinitz, B., ed. *Central City Economic Development.* Cambridge: Abt Books, 1979.

Colman, W. G. *Cities, Suburbs, and States: Governing and Financing Urban America.* New York: Macmillan Publishing Co., Inc., 1975.

Houseman, G. L. *The Right of Mobility.* Port Washington, N.Y.: Kennikat Press, 1979.

Inman, R. P. "Toward a National Urban Policy—Critical Reviews, Federal Policy and the Urban Poor," *Journal of Regional Science.* Vol. 19, No. 1 (1979):119-129.

Nelson, K. P. *Recent Suburbanization of Blacks: How Much, Who, and Where.* Office of Economic Affairs, The Office of Policy Development and Research, U.S. Department of Housing and Urban Development. Washington, D.C.: U.S. Government Printing Office, 1979.

Norton, R. D. *City Life-Cycles and American Urban Policy.* New York: Academic Press, Inc., 1979.

Norton, R. D. "Re-Industrialization and the Urban Underclass," paper contributed to the President's Commission for a National Agenda for the Eighties, Washington, D.C., 1980.

U.S. Department of Housing and Urban Development. *The President's National Urban Policy Report.* Washington, D.C.: U.S. Government Printing Office, 1978.

U.S. Department of Housing and Urban Development. *The President's National Urban Policy Report.* Washington, D.C.: U.S. Government Printing Office, 1980.

Chapter 6

Reappreciating
THE ROLE OF THE
States

The 20th-century deconcentration of residences and workplaces has strained the historical relationships among levels of government within our federal system. Coincident with this trend has been the concentration of power in and the assignment of increasing responsibilities to ever higher levels of government. This phenomenon is reflected in the remarkable growth of the public sector—first at the federal level and later at the local and state levels.

Although many extralocal governmental bureaucracies (state, regional, national) have grown exceedingly capable and influential in the past several decades, the 1970s witnessed a conscious effort to decentralize certain responsibilities for funding and administration from the federal to the local level. Thus, whether our focus is the centralizing dynamic of the period spanning the New Deal to the Great Society, or the decentralizing dynamic of New Federalism, one discovers that federal-local relationships have been continuously shaped and reshaped. As a result, local governments have become responsible for some functions previously reserved for higher levels of government, but have only highly variable capacities to assume them.

Considerable analysis has been made of the relationship between governmental structure and social and economic conditions. The issue often becomes when and under what conditions, not whether, the federal government should aid local governments. However, as legal entities, cities are the creations of states. Therefore, any policy with implications for local governmental structure and functioning should also involve state governments.

A More Visible Role for States

States specify, by charter or articles of incorporation, which powers localities may exercise and to what extent. Cities retain only those powers explicitly granted. States establish local governmental boundaries, functions, and revenue sources. They constrain annexation processes, determine the locations of major capital expenditure projects and development investments, and apportion the financial responsibilities for welfare and education among substate jurisdictions. States define the public services that localities provide, mandate their levels, and dictate municipal tax arrangements, including type, rate, and permitted exemptions. As the "constitutional parent of local government," states often unknowingly reinforce, through commission as well as omission, a large portion of the circumstances that cities must cope with. For instance, most states assume little responsibility for financing local education, shifting these burdens onto often strained local property tax bases. Yet, states are often woefully tardy in reforming the administration of the property tax, especially with respect to uniform full-value assessment. Furthermore, not only do a fifth of the states lack a state income tax, but states historically have forbidden localities to adopt a commuter tax or an income tax to bolster their revenue-generating capabilities.

Federal urban policy cannot afford to bypass and ignore states. A key to policy interventions that can restructure the incentives, opportunities, and constraints under which localities operate is found at the state level of government. However, only a very few states currently are willing or politically disposed to assume significantly greater responsibilities for cities in their jurisdictions, despite their increased capability to do so.

Rectifying inattentiveness and inadequacy at the state level might well be considered a major thrust of federal policy interventions in the decade ahead. Ambitious state action is required to modernize the structures, the revenue sources, and the service responsibilities of local governments in urban areas. The federal government could create the incentives for states to undertake these efforts.

What might state governments do? In the most general terms, states should turn to two tasks. First, they should consider providing direct financial assistance to distressed citizens and jurisdictions to ameliorate the distress conditions for which they are partly responsible. Second, they should allow, and indeed encourage, the revision of local government fiscal bases. More specifically, states could assume responsibility for some services historically assigned to local governments (elementary and secondary education, welfare). They could establish systems of statewide revenue sharing and categorical assistance to distressed localities, and encourage metropolitan tax-base sharing where annexation is no longer feasible or desirable.

States should review the property tax system, reexamining, for example, user charges for selected municipal services as an alternative to the excessive reliance by most communities on the property tax. States could help localities weigh the merits of contracting for the private provision of some traditional public services. Because local

governments often are accused of being "underbureau-
cratized," having neither the institutional nor the proce-
dural structures to manage services, property, land, or
finances efficiently, states could assist in modernizing
these facets of local government.

States could strengthen or modify local powers to
match the responsibilities for growth and decline management that localities have inherited. They could integrate
their own taxing powers and objectives more rationally
with those of substate jurisdictions. States could explore
the wide range of tax policies, regulations, legislation, and
incentive systems to ensure that local efforts are consistent
with development efforts among all substate urban and
rural areas.

Through inducements and constraints, states could influence the land-use policies now wielded largely for local
purposes; they also could seek to reassume certain land-use
control powers that have been delegated historically to localities. Through their regulatory and oversight capacities,
states could impose standards for a wide array of activities
common to all localities. Through the owning and acquisition of land, states could assume a more purposive role in
influencing the patterns of urban growth and decline.

In short, although urban problems do not respect the
jurisdictional boundaries of local governments, policy interventions aimed at urban problems do. Accordingly,
states should take the lead in adapting substate governments to the problems that are spilling beyond the boundaries of local municipalities. For those metropolitan areas
that spread over state boundaries, the same principle of an
increased policy presence for states should be employed
cooperatively between the affected states.

In reviewing the rather considerable powers of the states,
and their potential to craft comprehensive urban development policies to supplement, if not substitute for, federal
efforts, *The President's National Urban Policy Report*(s)
have noted the efforts already undertaken by selected
states across the country. Thirty-five states, along with
several dozen cities or metropolitan areas, have initiated
broadly based citizen efforts to anticipate and prepare for
growth and decline processes, and to harness the creative
energies of state-local partnerships to intervene in and to
influence the results of those processes.

Forty-two states provide preferential tax relief for
agricultural land and open space, 34 states are involved in
coastal zone management, 13 states have special legislation
protecting critical environmental areas, and 5 states require permits for developments with regional impacts.
Fifteen states have adopted new land-use legislation, and

**An
Appreciation
for Recent
Efforts**

nearly all 50 states have taken steps to bolster the state role in problems of land use and growth management. Colorado, Florida, Hawaii, Oregon, Maine, Massachusetts, Minnesota, North Carolina, and Vermont are in the vanguard of states that have assumed a major intervenor role in land-use management since the mid-1960s.

The intergovernmental structures and processes linking federal and local levels of government are key entry points into the urban policy process. Since states should be brought into full partnership with other levels of government, fiscal relationships provide an opportunity for that process to begin.

The most important category of revenue growth for local governments has been intergovernmental aid. Direct federal aid to local governments has grown dramatically in recent years. General and countercyclical revenue sharing, local public works funding, and Comprehensive Employment and Training Act (CETA) programs have become bonds of dependence as well as conduits for funds to local areas. Because the federal budget is increasingly subject to trimming and most state budgets are reporting surpluses, the time is right for states to become more actively involved in the functioning and financing of local governments. No uniform strategy can be suggested for all states, because the number of functions performed by local governments and the fiscal arrangements necessary to perform them vary considerably. Nonetheless, the character of a state government and its relationships to local and federal levels of government should be a major focus during the coming decade.

Advisory Commission on Intergovernmental Relations. *State Community Assistance Initiatives: Innovations of the Late '70s.* Washington, D.C.: U.S. Government Printing Office, 1979.

Litvak, L. and Daniels, B. *Innovations in Development Finance.* Washington, D.C.: Council of State Planning Agencies, 1979.

National Academy of Public Administration and the U.S. Advisory Commission on Intergovernmental Relations. "The States and Distressed Communities: Indicators of Significant Actions." Washington, D.C.: Office of Community Planning and Development, U.S. Department of Housing and Urban Development, 1979, working paper.

Pierce, N. R., Hagstrom, J., and Steinbach, C. *Democratizing the Development Process.* Washington, D.C.: Council of State Planning Agencies, 1979.

Schwartz, G. G. *Bridges to the Future: Forces Impacting Urban Economies.* Columbus, Ohio: The Academy for Contemporary Problems, 1978.

U.S. Department of Housing and Urban Development. *The President's National Urban Policy Report.* Washington, D.C.: U.S. Government Printing Office, 1978.

U.S. Department of Housing and Urban Development. *The President's National Urban Policy Report.* Washington, D.C.: U.S. Government Printing Office, 1980.

Vaughan, R. J. *State Taxation and Economic Development.* Washington, D.C.: Council of State Planning Agencies, 1979.

Warren, C. R. "Executive Summary: The States and Urban Strategies: A Comparative Analysis." Washington, D.C.: Office of Policy Development and Research, U.S. Department of Housing and Urban Development, 1980.

References

Chapter 7

RESPONDING TO A CHANGING URBAN AMERICA: TOWARD A
New Federal Policy Role

Because of the ongoing transformation of our central cities and the current deconcentration trends influencing that transformation, our nation's cities are experiencing economic and fiscal distress, while their residents are suffering from social distress. Such overall urban distress has invited a sequence of vigorous federal responses. As a result, for two decades the national government has developed its urban policy on a program-by-program basis and with a locational focus. But is this form of response appropriate?

To answer that question, several background queries need to be answered: What should be the ultimate concern of federal urban policy—people or places? How should federal policy responses be targeted? How responsive are the present allocational mechanisms? How should the urban impacts of nonurban federal policies be addressed? Finally, is a national urban policy, as it is currently conceived and implemented, the appropriate federal response to urban problems? Such questions are explored in this chapter.

The diversity of problems afflicting the nation's cities and their governments, businesses, and residents reflect long-term changes unfolding across several spatial scales—cities, suburbs, nonmetropolitan areas, multistate regions. This situation has recently invited remedy through broad-gauge urban policies and programs administered by a centralized policy machinery. Nevertheless, federal initiatives in urban policy have always been hobbled by the choice between two approaches: to help people directly or to aid them indirectly by helping local places, governments, and businesses directly. The people-versus-place orientation, although in some sense a phantom distinction because of the interdependence of the two, nonetheless has been a salient issue in urban policies of the past two decades.

Historically a general place orientation in federal urban policy has been the unavoidable consequence of the way political power is tied to and reflects political representation by Congressional districts. In general terms, Congressional

**People-
Versus-Place
Orientations**

support for urban policy initiatives is often the net result of the activities of all those who believe that a proposal benefits their district, state, or region, versus those who judge that it does not. Such political calculations unavoidably reflect a certain ultimate concern for the fates and fortunes of specific places. Understandably, the political system therefore has had great difficulty dealing with a truly national issue without first translating it into countless, narrow parochial issues, because eventually political support and votes will be tied to local and regional calculations of self-interest.

The contemporary commitment to a dominant place orientation in recent urban policy reflects both the structure of our political system and the experience of past policy initiatives. Even during times of unparalleled prosperity, pockets and even regions of disadvantage and distress have persisted. General macroeconomic policies have been unable to eliminate the poverty and distress of particular places. Fiscal and monetary policies have not been sufficiently surgical to root out and ameliorate localized distress. Likewise, transfer payments of aid, which so often are allocated to people and local governments on the basis of many factors other than need, also have been unable to eliminate distress in the midst of prosperity.

By default, yet consistent with the decentralization of federal power begun in the early 1970s, the backbone of federal urban policy initiatives has become a narrowly circumscribed concept of local economic development. There has been great emphasis placed on revitalizing specific places by stimulating local participation and leveraging private sector resources, with the assumption that alleviating the distress of specific places also would alleviate the distress of people in due course. Although instances of success do exist, the results for most distressed localities have not been encouraging. A wide variety of federal assistance programs are underused by distressed localities, owing in part to the insignificance of the size of the aid, a limited awareness of the programs' existence, a reluctance to depend on the federal government as a working partner, the regulation strings attached to federal money, and the aura of uncertainty concerning future funding or policy goals.

Arising out of the current federal policy emphasis on aiding specific places is the need for a method to identify those places requiring assistance. The favored approach is the notion of targeting. What is the aim? The identification and amelioration of need—an extremely illusive target for any policy effort.

Need Assessment and the Targeting of Federal Aid

72

No satisfying overall definition exists of what constitutes "need" in urban society, nor is it likely that one ever will. In its absence, proxy indicators must suffice. Urban need has three major dimensions: social, economic, and fiscal, which correspond roughly to the problems experienced by people, businesses, and local governments. "Social need" may be present if high proportions of the residents in a place are living in poverty, experiencing high rates of unemployment, or living in a location characterized by poor housing, poor schools, and high crime rates. Likewise, "economic need" may be experienced if cities have difficulty maintaining their economic bases because businesses do not expand in place or because they transfer part or all of their activities to alternative locations in the metropolitan area, in the region, to other regions, or out of the country altogether. "Fiscal need" may be identified if cities experience a growing imbalance between expenditure requirements and revenue-raising capabilities. Perennially imbalanced budgets, large debts, high taxes, low liquidity, and low bond ratings, as well as public service packages that do not reflect current service needs and a declining capability to meet those needs—all are symptoms of fiscal need.

Although these various needs may be interrelated, they do not necessarily occur together all of the time. Social needs have been most severe in southern cities, regardless of size, and in large midwestern cities. Economic needs tend to be concentrated in large northeastern and midwestern cities. Fiscal needs are most pronounced in medium and large southern and northeastern cities and in large midwestern cities.

Given these circumstances, choosing one dimension or even combinations of urban need to target federal aid to distressed people, places, and local governments is difficult. In addition, specification of targets by need will continue to be hampered by the lack of definitional consensus; by a lack of timely, accurate, and relevant data; and by the necessary adoption of general indicators at the sacrifice of useful details that are so important to understanding the problems of people, businesses, and local governments in specific places.

The concept of targeting has broad appeal as a policy symbol because federal resources for urban problems are quite modest and have been declining in real dollar terms since the late 1970s. Funds allocated through targeting are intended to achieve greater efficiency and equity through redistribution. The search for redistributive equity through the unequal treatment of people or places exhibiting unequal need is reasonably well appreciated, despite the political tendency to distribute scarce funds relatively broadly. However, the search for allocative efficiency is clouded in ambiguity. A politically (if not necessarily economically) efficient allocation of resources is often judged to be achieved in one of two ways—by putting the money where it will do the most good, or by putting the money where it is most needed. Clearly, the allocations across localities achieved by these different strategies need not, and most likely never will, be identical.

To date, some evidence exists to suggest that funds can be reasonably well targeted. Limited federal resources have been successfully directed to places where the needs are greatest, as measured by the accepted need assessment tools. However, this result may simply mean that once the decision is made about where to aim, the funds seem to get to the desired locations. This outcome says nothing about whether the selected allocation pattern and associated outcomes are the most efficient, effective, or even a marginal improvement over other possible distributions.

Another point should be appreciated: The funds available to allocate are so inadequate relative to the identified needs, and the underlying theories of local economic and community development and revitalization are so rudimentary, that even totally efficient targeting may have no substantial effect in slowing down the transformation of our nation's urban places. This latter realization, it would appear, is crucial. All others may be derivative or secondary.

Federal Aid Allocation Mechanisms

The dominant place orientation of current urban policies is dependent on a targeting capability that uses territorially defined localities (cities, metropolitan areas, counties, states, regions) as units of analysis. Even though in many cases the ultimate goal of federal urban policies is to aid people indirectly by aiding places directly, a place-oriented federal policy strategy depends on the capacity to identify and to direct resources to selected localities. The distribution pattern of federal funds to specific places, and the more obscure pattern of urban results in these places, are critically dependent on the mechanisms used to allocate federal resources.

In the past two decades, two principal mechanisms for allocating federal aid have been used—project grants and formula grants. Project grants distribute funds on a competitive or discretionary basis, where both the discretion and the competition remain largely at the federal level. Consequently, successful applicants must use the funds for relatively specific and predetermined purposes. Formula grants, on the other hand, reduce federal discretion, because local eligibility is specified by law or regulation. The allocative mechanism is a formula that guides the distribution of funds according to the distribution of some other resource (such as population) or circumstance (such as the unemployment rate). The competition and discretion surrounding alternative uses for these funds are shifted more toward the local levels of government.

74

Formula grants break down into three types—categorical, block, and unrestricted. Categorical grants involve a formula that directs funds to relatively narrowly defined uses, such as law enforcement assistance. Block grant formulas, such as community development block grants (CDBGs), allocate funds for more generic purposes, and the specifics are hammered out at the local level. Unrestricted funds, such as general revenue sharing (GRS), are distributed to the local level for relatively general purposes.

Currently, there are nearly 150 formula-based categorical grants to state and local governments; 130 of these are based on some measure of need. Formula-based grants together distribute nearly $50 billion annually to state and local governments. The formulas vary, depending on the intended uses for the funds. Many use a single factor such as population to allocate funds. Others use combinations of factors with differential weights in order to calibrate the kinds of effects desired on the chosen targets.

In the past decade, Congress has shifted away from reliance on scattered categorical grants. Recent emphasis has been on a few, large block and unrestricted grants (CDBG, GRS, and CETA), thus altering the character and substance of federal programmatic intervention into urban affairs.

The evolution of the federal strategy of "government by formula" places great weight on a very weak plank—how need is identified. Any conclusion about the fairness of allocations depends on prior specification of goals and on the choice of the proxy indicators of need that are used to construct the formula. In addition, formula-based aid strategies are only superficially objective and mechanistic, because the act of targeting is basically political. The truth of that allegation is seen most clearly when attempts are made to tamper with original formulas, retargeting them to achieve different allocation outcomes.

Responsiveness and Effectiveness of Federal Allocations

The urban impacts of federal assistance depend not only on the method of allocating resources, but also on where the resources are directed and how they are used. For example, substantial proportions of the funds distributed by formula go directly to local governments. Several notable consequences are associated with this allocation strategy. First, such arrangements often bypass state governments under the assumption that the federal and local levels of government better understand local needs and are "closer" to the people. This situation makes it extremely difficult for states to aid in bringing coherence to the multiple and varied development activities across substate units or to reorient their planning focus to metropolitan areas rather than localities.

A second consequence of this local government focus is that localities are often used to carry out national policy goals implicitly even though the federal funds received are not sufficient. The temptation also exists to recreate the organizational complexity of the federal bureaucracy at local and state levels simply to achieve a mesh between the respective bureaucracies.

Although cities in general benefit from these allocative arrangements, the political reality dictates that scarce resources are dispersed over a large number of jurisdictions. The consequence of this action is that any potential potency that might be realized in a concentrated form is diluted as resources are spread thinly throughout the nation. The structure of political power, not need in any of its traditional manifestations, becomes the template for distributing federal funds. The federal capacity to concentrate assistance for those people or places exhibiting the greatest distress thus is weakened. Indeed, the limited capacity of federal funds to ameliorate the consequences of major trends in this country is being squandered by the very allocational and political arrangements that make them available.

The policy of spreading funds across all jurisdictions combined with the economic and demographic deconcentration of the past decades has resulted in a shift of political power away from large central cities to the advantage of suburbs and small cities. For example, in recent years, the number of recipient jurisdictions has increased 40 percent, but available funds have risen by only 15 percent. Although in general more federal funds have been directed to cities by formula grants than project grants, the traditional categorical grant programs, which have lost much of their popularity, distribute more resources to cities (especially large cities) than block grant programs.

Federal policies that marry a place orientation with a formula allocative mechanism almost dictate that funds will be diluted to the disadvantage of the most distressed people and the most distressed places. Funds end up being available to people and places that have relatively less need. The moral authority undergirding national goals can often become eclipsed by more localized agendas. In addition, the more politically popular, formula-based block grant instruments can undermine the original purpose of spending federal money on those people and on those places that are in the most need.

During this century, industrial and household deconcentration from cities has proceeded on a nationwide level. Federal policies did not initiate these deconcentration processes, but they have increased the pace and broadened the scale at which they have unfolded. Employment and population growth—drawn from central cities to suburban and non-metropolitan areas in the Industrial Heartland, to the West, and more recently to the South—were marginally reinforced by a wide range of federal policies. In this sense the urban impacts of the federal policies implemented by some 2,000 bureaus, agencies, and administrations have unleashed a wide variety of largely inadvertent spatial tilts (favoring some places over others) and other urban impacts. For example, the billions of dollars spent on federal efforts via expenditure policies, the tax structure, subsidies, and regulatory policies, although locationally "blind," often exacerbate rather than ameliorate intra- and inter-regional disparities. "Taken together, these unintended consequences can and do swamp the impacts of the explicit programs designed to relieve regional distress."[1]

Increasingly, the patterns of direct federal outlays to places, people, or local governments can be monitored to appreciate better how the federal presence leads to intended and unintended consequences for urban America. Federal policies and programs may both exacerbate and alleviate the problems of people, places, and local governments. Federal nonurban policies, such as interstate highway construction and homeowner mortgage interest tax deductions, have had more telling urban impacts than explicit urban policies. Unfortunately, any one policy or program may simultaneously have desirable and undesirable urban impacts.

In aggregate, federal policies have contributed to the deconcentration of employment and the growing concentration of poor minorities in central cities, but they have not been the dominant influence. Other factors have been more powerful—market forces, transforming techniques of production (air conditioning; land-intensive physical plants; and a rapid decline in the costs of data transmittal, storage, and processing), general affluence, changing size and composition of households, and quality-of-life considerations. On balance, federal urban economic policies have probably had a relatively minor influence on changing patterns of economic growth, development, and decline.

Federal policies have impacts and influence on at least four domains. Of particular concern are the influences that policies and programs might have, inadvertently or not, on employment, household and personal income, the size and distribution of the population, and the fiscal circumstances of subnational governments. First, general impacts are created by the overall orientation of national policies, such as the waxing and waning of concern for "guns versus butter." Such shifts in emphases have diffuse consequences for the more specific policies and programs and the levels at which they are funded.

A second broad-scale influence results in changing relative prices generally throughout the national economy.

The imposition of wage and price controls, implementation of wage or price subsidies in one or more sectors, and the regulation of a wide variety of industries are examples of federal interventions that affect the price, and therefore the supply, of goods and services throughout the nation.

At a finer level of analysis, federal influence can result from targeting resources to localities for the purpose of overcoming a place-oriented deficiency, such as the incapacity of the local revenue base to adapt to changing socioeconomic conditions. Finally, more surgical federal impacts arise from efforts to alter relative prices within localities, which are illustrated by the provision of subsidized housing, transportation services, or public employment programs in communities where need has been demonstrated.

In general, aggregate federal outlays can be traced to urban impacts that reflect the long-run direction of underlying economic and demographic trends. Despite much popular consternation suggesting otherwise, the federal budget is "pro-city," if only slightly, because cities receive proportionally more funds than if the allocations were dictated only by the location of population. Thirty-six percent of federal outlays are allocated to cities of over 50,000 population, even though only 31 percent of the nation's population reside in them. It has been reported that:

> [T]he distribution of total federal outlays appears to have a "neutral" effect on different types of cities, whether characterized by rate of growth, unemployment rate, per capita income, or index of urban conditions. However, medium-sized cities and central cities typically receive more funds per capita than large and small cities, and suburban cities, respectively.[2]

If the distribution of total federal outlays is examined by region, the disparities (paced by person-oriented relief or national defense) between various regions grew between 1970 and 1976, with federal resources going disproportionately to cities in the South and West. Relief and human capital development outlays were the most inequitably distributed between 1970 and 1976, with portions of the Industrial Heartland receiving the least benefits. However, the distributional inequities between southern and northern cities are eclipsed by those within each region.

Out of this situation arises one important policy issue that must be faced: Whether the panoply of federal policies that have been crafted for purposes other than explicit urban outcomes and that have spatial consequences outweighing those of specifically urban and regional policies should somehow be tailored to achieve more desirable locational outcomes? For instance, should environmental regulations, investment tax credits, homeowner tax deductions, and other federal tax policies (all of which have narrow sectoral aims as their principal purpose) be manipulated so that they give greater stress to their locational consequences? It might be unfeasible and undesirable to bend these nonurban federal policies to serve predominantly urban economic development objectives.

The federal government spends billions of dollars annually in efforts to relieve social, economic, and fiscal distress throughout the nation. Even as those resources have increased, knowledge of the interconnections among the industrial, residential, and public sectors has sensitized us to the fact that attempts to ameliorate deficiencies and to lessen the intra- and interregional disparities often are exacerbated by the net impacts of an uncoordinated and incoherent federal presence. Tracing the direct effects on each individual sector is difficult enough; accounting for the significance of secondary and indirect impacts turns an analytic exercise into a captivating art form.

Explicit federal urban policies are probably less important to what happens in or near our nation's cities than the panoply of federal social service programs, income redistribution programs, tax policies, intergovernmental transfers, and macroeconomic policies (which affect the availability and cost of the several factors of production in the national economic system and alter the levels of demand for the goods and services produced). The economic and demographic geography of the nation is probably transforming with only minimal guidance by explicit federal urban policy.

The influence of the federal government on urban America is important to identify and monitor, if not because it is ultimately so decisive, then certainly because it is so diffuse. Its potential to reinforce the underlying demographic and economic dynamics shaping urban America far exceeds its potential to determine what urban America will become. Its potential to reinforce and, in some limited way, condition the flow of private sector resources likely exceeds its ability to use public funds to reach goals independently.

A National Urban Policy Reassessed

For better or for worse, this nation did not have an explicit national urban policy until *The President's National Urban Policy Report* was prepared in 1978. As the cumulative effects of economic and demographic shifts on the nation's communities were discerned with increasing clarity, the national nature of the identified problems seemed to necessitate a centrally coordinated and administered urban policy response. Those localities and regions in which economic vitality had been dampened and economic dependence had accumulated increasingly sought compensation for the locational biases of past and present nonurban federal policies as if they had determined, rather than merely rein-forced, larger dominant trends. Responsive to that senti-ment, the national urban policy report was the first major effort to rectify decades-old policy incoherence and incon-sistency. It also employed an explicit concern for distribu-tion of government resources and results in assessing the consequences of governmental activity.

The very notion of a "national urban policy" only gained currency and acquired a sense of urgency as a result of interest established within Congress at the beginning of the 1970s. Nonetheless, to the extent that the actions and inactions of the federal government have had inadvertent and unintended urban consequences, this nation has had a *de facto* urban policy for many years, albeit implicit, in-coherent, and fraught with internal contradictions. The desire to substitute an explicit for an implicit federal urban policy is neither surprising nor inconsistent with our na-tional experience in other policy domains. It remains to make some judgment about the wisdom of that substitu-tion and about the substance of the resultant policy.

The implicit national urban policy that has existed for decades can be viewed as the legacy of repeated attempts to achieve specific goals in innumerable problem areas within subsectors of the society and the economy. There has sel-dom been anything unitary or integrated, coordinated or coherent, about the urban aims of the myriad federal activ-ities. The constituent parts of these policies aimed at effecting urban outcomes can be sensibly grouped only by their consequences for our nation's communities and for those who reside in them, and not by the careful articulation of their intentions. This grouping of policies by consequence, if not by intention, mirrors the fragmentation of political power and decisionmaking in this nation, the inherited structure of political jurisdictions, the allocation of func-tions among levels of government, and a feature of our political culture related to the tension existing between the public and private sectors.

Ironically, the challenge to craft a unified and coherent national urban policy has been accepted during an unlikely period: A bewildering variety of urban circumstances have come to be defined as urban problems and thus the proper targets of collective attention; the limits of our knowledge and understanding in all areas are increasingly apparent; and competing territorially defined and sociodemo-graphic constituencies are most developed and articulate. Never before has the nation been able to make less of a claim to being plagued by a uniform set of urban prob-lems. Only the most general prescriptions relating to the desirability of a vital and growing national economy as a context within which our nation's local economies can function appears to make sense in the face of the great diversity of problems affecting different people and places throughout the country.

Proponents of an explicit national urban policy suggest that the very existence of an implicit national urban policy and the inefficiencies resulting in policy gaps and overlaps, competing and contradictory urban outcomes, and unintended and unwanted consequences demand attention. Coordination, coherence, and consistency are required if the public sector is to fulfill its historic function of ameliorating, supplementing, or otherwise correcting the mosaic of undesirable urban outcomes that result from the activity of the private sector. The centralized political economy must derive its strength from coordination if it is to alter the urban outcomes of the decentralized private economy.

Some opponents of a national urban policy base their arguments not on the inappropriateness of consistency and coherence as policy goals or on the federal government as an urban policy initiator or implementer, but rather on the futility of the enterprise. This nation is overwhelmingly urban, but this fact is not the consequence of characteristics of places wherein people reside, but of the fact that the nation's culture is urban centered. "Place" makes all the difference politically, but ever less difference socially or economically. Poverty, unemployment, institutional discrimination, and fiscal insufficiency, among other undesirable conditions, are found in all regions and in all types of communities. Any hope of attending to the problems of people in places directly demands a detailed understanding of both the specific people and the specific places.

Incomplete understanding of the influences shaping our national settlements is matched by an array of inevitably imperfect policy tools. Further, public policy interventions have been and will continue to be relatively impotent in the face of processes whose casual mechanisms are not fully understood. Considering the great emphasis placed on coordination of federal efforts, care should be taken to avoid overselling such management strategies. Inappropriate policy instruments in the service of inappropriate policy goals, no matter how well organized, will prove to be ineffectual, if not manifestly detrimental.

Many uniform urban policies administered centrally will probably be irrelevant to specific problems in specific places; many urban policies administered via decentralization will also fail. A major reassignment of functions to the national and subnational governments and a reorientation toward policies that help people directly while allowing the nation's communities to transform should be considered.

Finally, the proper role of the federal government in urban policy areas needs to be carefully examined. Movements of capital, income, people, and jobs, which simultaneously benefit some places and burden others, are as inevitable as they are essential to the health and vitality of the national economy and society. What should be the federal government's role with respect to subnational development and equity issues, considering its responsibility for the functioning of the large national system?

If the *intermediate* goal is to direct greater concentrations of federal resources toward cities to ease their transition to new forms and to facilitate their performance of new functions, it will continue to make more sense to retarget by adjusting our current formula mechanisms, than to attempt to obtain an altered spatial distribution of federal outlays by abandoning the formula grant strategy in favor of some other allocation mechanism. Formulas should be regeared to distribute federal largesse, including the large, relatively unrestricted block grants, more on the basis of need, as well as to reward those political jurisdictions whose local tax efforts indicate that they are doing all they can to achieve enhanced community and economic development.

Beyond this, the federal government should prepare to turn the leadership of subnational development over to states and localities. It should strive to nurture the kind of flexibility that will allow and encourage different states and localities to define their problems and policy prescriptions differently. The federal government should concentrate its efforts on maintaining the most robust national economy possible. It should take the initiative in urban aid programs to view the nation as a unified whole rather than as a mosaic of interregional and intrametropolitan conflicts in need of federal resolution. It should assist transforming localities in their often painful growth or shrinkage to achieve new balances between employment and population. Finally, it should commit itself through its moral capacities and material resources to alleviating the distress of people directly, wherever they may live in this nation.

More importantly, if the *ultimate* goal is to direct greater concentrations of federal resources directly to people, wherever they may live, rather than indirectly to people through places and political jurisdictions, a national urban policy sensitive to distribution patterns might best be recast into more coherent national economic and social policies. As understanding of the root causes of distress and the possibilities and limitations of centralized policy initiatives deepens, our national responses to problems that are found in all communities also should evolve—from a largely place-oriented, locationally sensitive, national urban policy, to more people-oriented, locationally neutral, national economic and social policies.

Finally, and most telling of all, because of the complexity of the issues, the nation shies away from weighing

Transitional and Long-Term Policy Prescriptions

82

competing values in the context of difficult choices. By far, the most troublesome urban problems constituting individual and institutional distress can be traced to deconcentration trends that can be judged beneficial by alternative criteria. But what actions should the federal government take when the majority may already be benefitting from trends that public policies may not be able to influence?

> Society cannot simply decide to change the form and character of cities to make them conform to rationally determined aims and orders of priorities. . . . Social agencies that tinker with the form and character of the city cannot, therefore produce much . . . for the force behind such readjustment plans is pathetically small compared with the tremendous pressures exerted by the economy and technological capacity. Profound changes in the character of the city can only come from the sources from which they have always come, changes in economy and technology.[3]

Federal Urban Policy: Flexibility and Focus

No remedy to a set of circumstances deemed undesirable and defined as a "problem" is likely to make sense forever. Not only the circumstances and the criteria that define a problem change, but also the notions as to what constitutes a successful solution change. "[P]redictably . . . urban policy has failed to do what it could not be expected to do. Saving older cities as downtown enclaves does little if anything for the bottom third of the city population. Only more direct people-oriented policies can help the urban poor."[4]

A place-oriented national urban policy that becomes bogged down by being the instrumentality for mediating, if not instigating, interregional and intrametropolitan competition may not have as its primary goal the fortunes of people living in the nation's communities as they experience largely immutable demographic, economic, cultural, and technological changes. In this light, the contemporary place orientation in federal urban policy has probably done as much for us as it is likely to do.

In the context of demographic and economic deconcentration at all spatial scales, people-oriented policies on incomes, manpower, and social services should be articulated better. Also needed are a positive government-business partnership to develop policy for the nation's industrial sectors, a system of national economic planning, and a national science policy to promote economic growth derivative from our competitive strengths in an international economy. A sensitivity to local and regional concerns should be subordinated to promoting the vitality of the

83

larger economic system and mediating the adjustments that places and people must eventually accommodate.

A mix among policy and program results of frequent failures and serendipitous successes may have less to do with depleted public coffers than with depleted imagination, less to do with a deficiency of will and good intentions than with a distinct policy orientation that is not fully acknowledged. That traditional orientation is characterized by the tilting of a relatively inadequate federal policy presence against a sweep of developments whose potency and scope are underestimated, whose substance is not fully understood, and whose significance is too quickly appreciated in negative terms. The nation must be willing to look at old or changing circumstances in new ways.

Notes

1. L. M. Salamon and J. Helmer, "Urban and Community Impact Analysis: From Promise to Implementation," in *The Urban Impacts of Federal Policies,* ed., N.J. Glickman (Baltimore: Johns Hopkins University Press, 1980), p. 33.
2. G. Vernez, "Overview of the Spatial Dimensions of the Federal Budget," in *The Urban Impacts of Federal Policies,* ed., N.J. Glickman (Baltimore: Johns Hopkins University Press, 1980), p. 90.
3. J. Roebuck, *The Shaping of Urban Society* (New York: Charles Scribner's Sons, 1974), p. 231.
4. R. D. Norton, "Re-industrialization of the Urban Underclass," paper contributed to the President's Commission for a National Agenda for the Eighties, Washington, D.C.: 1980, pp. 40-41.

References

Advisory Commission on Intergovernmental Relations. *Block Grants: A Comparative Analysis.* Washington, D.C.: U.S. Government Printing Office, 1977.

Advisory Commission on Intergovernmental Relations. *Categorical Grants: Their Role and Design.* Washington, D.C.: U.S. Government Printing Office, 1977.

Barro, S. M. *The Urban Impacts of Federal Policies: Vol. 3, Fiscal Conditions.* Santa Monica: Rand Corporation, 1978.

Bearse, P. "Toward a National Urban Policy—Critical Reviews, Influencing Capital Flows for Urban Economic Development: Incentives or Institution Building?" *Journal of Regional Science.* Vol. 19, No. 1 (1979):79-91.

Carter Administration. *Small Community and Rural Development Policy.* Washington, D.C.: U.S. Government Printing Office, 1980.

Chinitz, B., ed. *Central City Economic Development.* Cambridge: Abt Books, 1979.

Downs, A. "Key Issues Concerning the Long-Range Policies and Programs of the U.S. Department of Housing and Urban Development." Washington, D.C.: Office of Policy Development and Research, U.S. Department of Housing and Urban Development, 1977, working paper.

Downs, A. "Some Thoughts on Creating a 'National Urban Policy,'" testimony before the Subcommittee on Intergovernmental Relations, Committee on Governmental Affairs, U.S. Senate, Washington, D.C., 1978.

Glickman, N. J. "National Urban Policy in an Age of Economic Austerity," report contributed to the President's Commission for a National Agenda for the Eighties, Washington, D.C., 1980.

Glickman, N. J., ed. *The Urban Impacts of Federal Policies.* Baltimore: Johns Hopkins University Press, 1980.

Menchik, M. D. *The Service Sector and Rural America: Issues for Public Policy and Topics for Research.* Santa Monica: Rand Corporation, 1980.

Morrison, P., Vaughan, R., Vernez, G., and Williams, B. *Recent Contributions to the Urban Policy Debate.* Santa Monica: Rand Corporation, 1979.

Nathan, R. P., Dommel, P. R., Liebschutz, S. F., Morris, M. D., and Associates, The Brookings Institution. *Block Grants for Community Development.* U.S. Department of Housing and Urban Development. Washington, D.C.: U.S. Government Printing Office, 1977.

National Transportation Policy Study Commission. *National Transportation Policies Through the Year 2000.* Washington, D.C.: U.S. Government Printing Office, 1979.

The President's Urban and Regional Policy Group, U.S. Department of Housing and Urban Development. *A New Partnership to Conserve America's Communities: A National Urban Policy.* Washington, D.C.: U.S. Government Printing Office, 1978.

Research and Policy Committee. *An Approach to Federal Urban Policy.* New York: Committee for Economic Development, 1977.

Reuss, H. S. *To Save Our Cities: What Needs to be Done.* Washington, D.C.: Public Affairs Press, 1977.

Subcommittee on the City, Committee on Banking, Finance, and Urban Affairs, U.S. House of Representatives, 95th Congress, First Session. *Toward a National Urban Policy.* Washington, D.C.: U.S. Government Printing Office, 1977.

Subcommittee on the City, Committee on Banking, Finance, and Urban Affairs, U.S. House of Representatives, 95th Congress, Second Session. *City Need and the Responsiveness of Federal Grants Programs.* Washington, D.C.: U.S. Government Printing Office, 1978.

U.S. Department of Housing and Urban Development. *Developmental Needs of Small Cities.* Washington, D.C.: U.S. Government Printing Office, 1977.

U.S. Department of Housing and Urban Development. *The President's National Urban Policy Report.* Washington, D.C.: U.S. Government Printing Office, 1978.

U.S. Department of Housing and Urban Development. *The President's National Urban Policy Report.* Washington, D.C.: U.S. Government Printing Office, 1980.

U.S. Department of Transportation. *National Transportation Trends and Choices (To the Year 2000).* Washington, D.C.: U.S. Government Printing Office, 1977.

Vaughan, R. J. *The Urban Impacts of Federal Policies: Vol. 2, Economic Development.* Santa Monica: Rand Corporation, 1977.

Vaughan, R. J. *Inflation and Unemployment: Surviving the 1980s.* Washington, D.C.: Council of State Planning Agencies, 1979.

Vaughan, R. J. and Vogel, M. E. *The Urban Impacts of Federal Policies: Vol. 4, Population and Residential Location.* Santa Monica: Rand Corporation, 1979.

Vining, D. R., Jr. "Toward a National Urban Policy—Critical Reviews, The President's National Urban Policy Report: Issues Skirted and Statistics Omitted," *Journal of Regional Science.* Vol. 19, No. 1 (1979):69-77.

Weinstein, B. L. and Clark, R. J. "Urban Trends and the Condition of Cities." Washington, D.C.: Southern Growth Policies Board, 1979, draft report.

Chapter 8

OVERCOMING THE LEGACY OF
Past Federal Urban
Policies: WHERE TO BEGIN

W e cannot expect the federal government to adopt overnight a new perspective on the nation's settlements and a new approach to ensure their adjustment to changing demographic and economic realities. While that period of careful reassessment of long-term federal urban policy objectives proceeds, critical and difficult first steps can be taken to lend greater coherence to current efforts. These steps should be viewed as part of a transitional policy and as necessary, but not sufficient, actions in the move toward a federal urban policy that makes greater sense for the coming decade and beyond. At best, they may facilitate progress toward a more sensible long-range urban policy, if for no other reason than because they sensitize the nation to the folly of continued tinkering and unchecked elaboration of present federal activities. It is time to gain some control over a policy apparatus that appears to drive us rather than respond to our commands.

This chapter begins by highlighting the importance of decongesting our system of intergovernmental relations, which has increasingly shifted responsibility and power within our federal system and distorted traditional distinctions within a local-state-federal division of labor. Among the consequences of a distorted federal system are a panoply of federal community and economic development programs that lack coordination and coherence. They exist to respond to idiosyncratic and isolated goals rather than working toward an integrated federal presence—a situation that is explored further in this chapter. Finally, there is much to be gained by considering the reassignment of traditional government functions across the several levels of government and between the public and private sectors.

Since the mid-1960s, the patterns of relationships between localities, counties, states, and the federal government have grown extremely complex, and the boundaries of their respective domains have lost meaning. Certain basic constraints in the constitutional, fiscal, and political

**Decongesting
an Overloaded
Intergovern-
mental
System[1]**   87

arenas have eroded. As a result, responsibilities for funding and administration of many governmental functions have become hopelessly intergovernmentalized. In short, the consequence of our current federal aid system, which has expanded dramatically, is overload. If the nation is to improve the effectiveness, efficiency, equity, and accountability of all three levels of government, the intergovernmental system should be decongested and a clear functional division of labor reimposed. This matter deserves careful attention because over the past decade, many urban problems have increasingly been handled by expanding reliance on intergovernmental strategies and mechanisms, while obscuring historical distinctions within the federal system.

The overload of the intergovernmental system can be diagnosed by several symptoms, including:

- ☐ Obliteration of the distinctions between private and public concerns.
- ☐ Loss of distinctions between federal and state-local areas of concern.
- ☐ Increasing dependence of state and local budgets on federal grants revenues.
- ☐ Use of state and local governments to implement national policies.
- ☐ Conversely, use of the federal government to further local or state concerns.

Given the recent hyper-responsiveness of the federal government, and particularly Congress, every narrow issue seems to reach the national agenda. "Presidents act almost as frequently in a mayoral or gubernatorial role as in a national Presidential one, and Congress plays a municipal and county council, not to mention the state legislative, role as often as it acts as a national deliberative body."[2] Incessant and intrusive intergovernmentalism is the inevitable result.

The size of the federal bureaucracy has not increased for some time, despite an ever mounting number of assignments given to it. In addition, no change has occurred in the federal government's almost exclusive reliance on intergovernmental grants as its primary mechanism for carrying out domestic responsibilities. This approach permits the national government to avoid some basic domestic governmental responsibilities while cluttering up its agenda with issues that properly belong to lower government levels. Neither equity (either interpersonal or interjurisdictional), nor administrative effectiveness, nor economic efficiency, nor above all political, electoral, or administrative accountability are enhanced by the tendency to intergovernmentalize practically all domestic questions, nearly all subnational governmental functions, and most of the national government's own civil governmental obligations.

The overloaded intergovernmental system has resulted in several problems. For example, the federal grant system itself has become overloaded. The current product is nearly 500 aid programs and the concomitant participation in dozens of policy domains where they previously played no roles. It has assumed policy leadership in virtually every functional field, including those traditionally the province of state and local governments. Opportunities for improving the grant system can be realized by program simplification and consolidation. In addition, a major reassignment of functions among levels of government could ease the grant system overload problem, eliminating the federal role and aid where the federal contribution is misplaced and/or minor.

Another problem has been the imposition of excessive costs on state and local governments. The continual and increasing use of grant and regulatory mechanisms imposes very expensive and difficult, although often initially hidden, costs on state and local governments. Although the tendency to ignore potential costs is most visible in overt regulatory law, it is equally true of the myriad national policy objectives and conditions now attached to grant programs.

Yet another problem is the neglect of state and local interests in the political process. Much governmental authority and power have shifted toward Washington, D.C., in the past two decades. The traditional, strongly decentralized political system has become heavily pluralistic and more national, with power organized more on a vertical and functional basis. The result is that state and local governments play a far less authoritative role in national policy decisions than before. The irony is that the heavy fiscal dependency of state and local governments on external funds makes it exceedingly unlikely that they will reassert themselves. This situation is especially true in a period defined by fiscal constraint and popular demands for state and local tax reductions.

Coordinating Federal Community and Economic Development Efforts[3]

Currently, the federal government administers some 300 community and economic development programs that tend to be *ad hoc,* incoherent, and inconsistent. The overall result of this condition is a fragmentation of occasionally necessary and worthwhile federal urban initiatives. The tremendous variation across regions and states (and even within metropolitan areas and cities) of the underlying economic problems is not yet fully appreciated. Although some observers suggest that the elegance and relative simplicity of general economic policies can be used to alleviate local economic distress, macroeconomic policies and those that are oriented toward the short-term use of transfer payments to places and people have not had the desired effects.

Macroeconomic policies and transfer payments are inadequate for several reasons. First, general macroeconomic policies tend to be too broadly gauged. Because they are aimed at national averages, they inevitably leave pockets of distress unattended. Transfer payments require a dispensing bureaucracy that over time gains both an innovation inertia and a growth momentum independent of the size of its task. As its size grows, its resources grow. The logical consequence of the dispersal of transfer funds is to create and nurture a growing addiction to and dependence on those federal resources that in the long run may be self-defeating. For example, the level of dependence on federal resources in the nation's 15 largest cities increased from 5.2 percent of local revenues in 1967 to 47.5 percent in 1978.

Because of the above limitations, the organizational structure and functioning of the major federal-local development programs require restructuring. The aim is to reconsider not only how programs are designed to achieve certain results, but also more fundamentally how the programs developed, what their patronage is within Congressional committees, what degree of support they receive from their well defined constituencies, and where they should be located in the federal bureaucracy.

The 300-odd programs can be clustered into three basic activities:

1. **General fiscal and monetary policies** (e.g., the budget, Federal Reserve actions), which affect the overall condition of the economy—the rate of economic growth, the extent of unemployment, and the level of prices;
2. **Transfer payments to individuals** (e.g., welfare aid, food stamps, Social Security payments, and unemployment compensation), which provide assistance directly to families and individuals in need; and
3. **Development assistance,** which provides financial aid to states, local governments, businesses, and individuals to construct public facilities, attract businesses, improve neighborhoods, provide training, upgrade housing conditions, and the like.[4]

Six major functional categories serve as policy domains for the above strategies: economic development, community development and public facilities investment, housing, transportation, employment and training, and development planning. In addition, eight different federal agencies administer the programs: the Department of Housing and Urban Development; the Economic Development Administration of the Department of Commerce; the Farmers Home Administration of the Department of Agriculture; the Small Business Administration; the Community Services Administration; the Title V Regional Action

Planning Commissions; the Department of Labor; and the Environmental Protection Agency.

Programs and resources are badly fragmented. The organizational arrangements that exist produce widespread duplication and confusion of functions. For example, the provision of economic development assistance to local businesses comes from at least a dozen programs administered by five governmental agencies. In addition, program procedures differ and sometimes conflict, federal delivery systems diverge widely, and lines of responsibility within the federal bureaucracy are blurred. No agency has overall responsibility for subnational development problems; there is no clear division of responsibilities along either functional or geographic lines.

The consequences of current arrangements are profound. Confusion and excessive administrative burdens and costs are created for state and local governments. Federal personnel and other resources are used in an inefficient manner. Not only do policy duplications exist, but also policy vacuums and gaps are apparent. These federal programs lack the flexibility required to respond to local needs and opportunities and to pool and focus limited funds. In addition, the programs involve unnecessary uncertainty and delays that discourage private sector participation. Fragmentation in local planning and programming efforts is almost guaranteed because local institutions have to work with a relatively uncoordinated and incoherent federal development bureaucracy. Because these programs cannot be easily compared and evaluated for effectiveness, the likelihood of their successful transfer from site to site is reduced. Because some nontraditional participants (such as nonprofit, community-based development organizations) have difficulty in gaining access to economic development assistance, their possible innovative activities are stifled or at least discouraged. A particularly regrettable legacy of this federal development assistance establishment is that certain remarkably creative and energetic local and state efforts are easily discouraged or distorted by the necessity of having to organize to interact with the uncoordinated and confusing federal establishment.

Possible ingredients of a more coherent and coordinated system include housing the scattered organizational and programmatic elements with development assistance as their main task under a single authority. Also, federal development assistance could be streamlined by consolidating major economic development grant and loan programs, development planning programs, and rural community facilities programs into their respective functional categories. Major candidates for consolidation could include community development block grants, urban development action grants, and Economic Development Administration grants. Another useful ingredient would be the greater coordination of the major federal development assistance efforts. Finally, place-oriented development assistance should be connected with federal, state, and local efforts in manpower policy.

Every level of government in a federal system has exclusive or shared responsibility for a wide variety of functions. Today, obvious deficiencies exist in the assignment of functions. An intergovernmental and intersectoral reassignment of governmental functions is essential for an effective federal urban policy presence in the short term, even while the national government reassesses the scope, substance, and orientation of its urban policy role over the long run.

Reassigning Functions Among Levels of Government and Between the Public and Private Sectors

The current intergovernmental arrangement focuses primary responsibility at the federal level. With certain exceptions, many of the functions that have flowed to the federal government in past decades might well be reassigned to other, lower levels of government. On the other hand, the federal government could take over some functions currently handled at subnational levels. For example, the federal government could take financial, if not administrative, responsibility for welfare and health insurance programs, because the nation has an obligation to assist the poor and the sick, regardless of where they were born or where they may now live.

In past decades, a number of factors have stimulated the growth of the federal government in scope, if not always in size, with important consequences in a wide variety of urban policy areas. Shifts in the population and economy have led to increasing activity in many federal programs. In an effort to maintain the real dollar benefit levels in many federal programs, automatic cost-of-living adjustments have been added. Past policy commitments often have had a snowball effect because new groups become eligible for federal assistance at higher benefit levels year after year. Finally, the unrelenting political tendency to inaugurate new programs, rather than supplement existing programs, has tended to expand the responsibilities of the federal government.

Sorting out functions among levels of government and the public and private sectors is a course of action that should be tackled promptly for a variety of reasons. First, the nature of certain services are such that a reallocation process would allow their delivery with greater economic efficiency, fiscal equity, political accountability, and administrative effectiveness. To be avoided during this process are: the failure to realize economies of scale, the imposition of uncompensated costs or benefits on other jurisdictions, the inability of a level of government to handle its responsibilities because of a lack of organizational sophistication or expertise, and the neglect of channels of citizen access, control, and participation.

Assignments that are inefficient court higher costs for lower quality and reduced scope. Assignments that are inequitable distribute costs and benefits unfairly across recipients. Assignments that are ineffective lead to illogical and uncoordinated performance patterns by governments. Assignments that are no longer accountable to recipients risk popular disaffection and resistance directed at government generally. The present *ad hoc* approach to allocating functional responsibilities exhibits all of these flaws.

Another reason for reassignment is the possibility of reducing the size and scope of federal budget expenditures after decades of federal growth. In the past quarter century, federal spending has grown from 18 percent to 22 percent of the gross national product. The historic shift of traditionally subnational functions to the federal government accounts for a major portion of that growth. Increasing assistance to state and local governments for an ever wider range of functions has also contributed to that growth.

Numerous responsibilities of the federal government may be performed better, and more properly, by state or local governments. Subnational governments may be more responsive to localized circumstances and may provide a more direct accounting to the electorate. They may also be more able to meet and control rising costs of services.

One major thrust of a transitional federal urban policy would be to assist state and local governments in working out divisions of labor that reflect more adequately the changing distribution of population groups; the altered adequacies of fiscal bases used by different levels of government; the changing technological requirements and possibilities accompanying different programs, public services, and their delivery systems; and the accumulated experience of governments at all levels in delivering services. Where the claim that the federal level of government is closest to the people in local jurisdictions can be substantiated, efforts might be made to encourage and assist states and localities to be more sensitive to this issue.

Little uniformity exists among or within states regarding what level and type of government has the responsibility for a particular function or any of its components. However, a pattern of centralization or decentralization of various services has emerged. These trends should be studied carefully to see whether or not a more defensible system of functional assignments is emerging naturally. In such instances, an intermediary and facilitative role might be useful for the federal government.

Accompanying the shift of functions away from the federal government should be a concern for the task of capacity building and the provision of technical assistance to subnational governments. These actions would ensure that as money and responsibility decentralize, the receiving level of government is both willing and capable of consistency with national goals while they work on their more localized agendas.

Certain negative consequences may arise from the reassignment process. The shift from categorical assistance toward block grants and automatic entitlements has effectively shifted much competition to local levels of government and increased local autonomy. In the process, the federal government has surrendered much potential leverage for ensuring that state and local actions are consistent with larger national goals. For example, the monies that come with fewer federal strings are likely to be more parochial and place-oriented than people-oriented.

In initiating the reassignment of governmental functions, the federal government should take a low-profile role where possible. Assistance and encouragement might be offered to states in return for their attention to and action in changing local and state patterns of functional assignment for which emerging support and logical justification exists. No single division of labor that is appropriate for all jurisdictions is evident; the federal role should be one of encouraging an ever greater fit with the needs and capabilities of regions or substate localities within states.

Another important form of reassignment of traditional governmental functions is possible—to the private sector. Although such a move would affect local functional assignments relatively directly and the agenda of federal responsibilities relatively indirectly, such intersector shifts do merit consideration. As localities shift some traditional functions to the private sector—by default, if not by design —they will be able to accommodate better new responsibilities evolving from above. The direct use of private sector provision of services, and the greater reliance on market principles in the performance of traditional governmental functions, has been growing, but only relatively recently.

The factors that account for the historical estrangement of the public and private sectors flow from an article of faith that the government does not exist to make a profit. Yet, this ethic is increasingly countered by a growing concern for accountability and efficiency in government. Greater reliance on voucher and incentive systems and simulated profit centers; greater concern for public pricing and the use of user fees; and the more frequent use of performance contracts between one level of government and the private sector all illustrate the gradually increasing attractiveness of importing, where feasible, the characteristics of the private market economy into the public political economy.

The divestment of selected functions to the private sector is a strategy that might be usefully integrated into a transitional federal urban policy. The skyrocketing cost of local government in the past two decades, the mounting evidence that private sector service provision is often superior to public provision, the intensified search for a yardstick against which to measure the performance of the public sector, as well as the realization that opportunities are being missed to develop an essentially untapped business sector—all of these factors are cogent justifications for an increased federal government effort in easing and guiding public-private divisions of labor into existence.

The larger task of designing and implementing a new federal urban policy presence can be aided significantly by first attending to the serious flaws that exist in present federal urban policy mechanisms and efforts. Consideration of these transitional steps provides an opportunity to reexamine and reassign functional responsibilities based on what is working well and on what could be working better. Such reassignments recognize that certain levels of government can no longer bear the burdens that have historically been assigned to them in a random and haphazard manner. Some government functions could benefit from being universalized, others from being more tailored to fit recipients and government capabilities, and still others from being assumed by the private sector.

1. This section of the chapter is based on: Advisory Commission on Inter-governmental Relations, *An Agenda for American Federalism: Restoring Confidence and Competence* (Washington, D.C.: U.S. Government Printing Office, forthcoming).
2. Ibid., p. 9.
3. This section of the chapter is based on: President's Reorganization Project, "Organizing for Development: Reorganization Study of Federal Community and Economic Development Programs" (Washington, D.C.: Office of Management and Budget, 1979, draft).
4. Ibid., p. 4.

Advisory Commission on Intergovernmental Relations. *Improving Urban America: A Challenge to Federalism.* Washington, D.C.: U.S. Government Printing Office, 1976.

Advisory Commission on Intergovernmental Relations. *Pragmatic Federalism: The Reassignment of Functional Responsibility.* Washington, D.C.: U.S. Government Printing Office, 1976.

Advisory Commission on Intergovernmental Relations. *The Dynamics of Growth: A Crisis of Confidence and Competence.* Washington, D.C.: U.S. Government Printing Office, 1980.

Advisory Commission on Intergovernmental Relations. "A System Overloaded: American Federalism 1959-1979," *Intergovernmental Perspective.* Washington, D.C.: ACIR, Vol. 6, No. 1 (Winter 1980).

Advisory Commission on Intergovernmental Relations. "What is the Future of Federalism," *Intergovernmental Perspective.* Washington, D.C.: ACIR, Vol. 6, No. 3 (Summer 1980).

Congressional Budget Office. *Reducing the Federal Budget: Strategies and Examples.* Washington, D.C.: U.S. Government Printing Office, 1980.

Miller, R. B. "The Federal Role in Cities: The New Deal Years," *Commentary.* Washington, D.C.: National Council for Urban Economic Development (July 1979): 11-13.

President's Reorganization Project. "Organizing for Development: Reorganization Study of Federal Community and Economic Development Programs." Washington, D.C.: Office of Management and Budget, 1979, draft report.

The President's Urban and Regional Policy Group, U.S. Department of Housing and Urban Development. *A New Partnership to Conserve America's Communities: A National Urban Policy.* Washington, D.C.: U.S. Government Printing Office, 1978.

Chapter 9

PERSPECTIVES
ON URBAN AMERICA AND
Key Policy Issues
FOR THE EIGHTIES

U ntil 50 years ago, the proper federal role vis-a-vis the nation's cities was easily summarized. Because the Constitution had not explicitly specified otherwise, the responsibility for cities devolved to state governments. With the onslaught of the Depression, the federal government began for the first time to consider cities as national, rather than merely state, assets. Accordingly, New Deal recovery policies included federal assistance for both distressed people and beleaguered local governments. The rationale behind this action was that "the American economy was dependent upon the health of the many urban industrial economies within it and that it was in the best interests of the federal government to aid those [local] economies."[1] This national economic calamity henceforth legitimized the appropriateness of a general federal urban policy presence, even though a commitment to continuing federal involvement in the functioning of local economies was never intended.

In the past 20 years, the time-honored logic of a federal commitment to assisting people in cities has been extended to assisting the cities as well. Welfare and income maintenance programs have been supplemented by programs that emphasize physical redevelopment, local economic development, and direct fiscal aid to local governments. The transition from the War on Poverty and Great Society era of the 1960s to the New Federalism of the 1970s did much to legitimize an increasing federal emphasis on places in the country. This emergent spatial sensitivity in public policy has become particularly apparent during the past 4 years, as illustrated by the dominant thrusts of the national urban policy and executive orders devoted to urban impact analysis, federal facility siting, and targeted procurement. The New Deal emphasis on helping distressed people in cities directly has evolved into an emphasis on helping distressed places (local business and government) directly for the purpose of helping people indirectly. Today most federal funds directed to urban problems go to "place" recipients rather than distressed people. In the late 1970s, a spatial sensitivity appears to have overtaken in large part a social sensitivity developed during the previous decade. Politically, this shift is justified by the assertion that aiding places with problems is easier than aiding people with problems. Economically, this shift is justified by the assertion that direct aid to local economies multiplies its impact so that benefits reverberate throughout the economy in ways that direct aid to people does not.

The 1980s may well require a new perspective on aiding distressed people in urban America. To import the 1930s rationale for a federal urban policy role across the decades may not be wise. Although the economy in the 1930s was indeed dependent on the health of local urban industrial economies in ways not fully appreciated, and it undoubtedly was in the best interest of the federal government to aid those local economies, circumstances have conspired to weaken that rationale.

Unlike a half-century ago, contemporary urban economies are no longer confined within the political jurisdictions of cities. Modern urban economies have an expanded scope that integrates central city, suburban, and nonmetropolitan economies. The deconcentration trends accompanying the arrival of a postindustrial era highlight the fact that the nation's economic vitality no longer arises from or is tied to specific types of places. It increasingly derives its strength from all kinds of places, both local political jurisdictions and beyond. Today it may be in the best interest of the nation to commit itself to the promotion of locationally neutral economic and social policies rather than spatially sensitive urban policies that either explicitly or inadvertently seek to preserve cities in their historical roles. A federal policy presence that allows places to transform and assists them in adjusting to difficult circumstances can justify shifting greater explicit emphasis to helping directly those people who are suffering from the transformation process.

Our cities are truly national assets. Hence, the federal policy presence should recognize that the health of a city, or any other settlement, is determined not by population or employment levels, but by its ability to perform vital functions for the larger society. As national assets, cities and their residents are the resources and responsibilities of us all during their adjustment to the postindustrial era. With this perspective in mind, a redefined federal policy role in urban America for the coming decade is presented.

The economic health of our nation's communities ultimately depends on the health of our nation's economy. Federal efforts to revitalize urban areas through a national urban policy concerned principally with the health of

A National Urban Policy Reconsidered

specific places will inevitably conflict with efforts to revitalize the larger economy. Federal efforts to nurture economic growth through increased productivity, expanded markets, job creation, and controlled inflation will require that settlements, their residents, and local governments adjust to changing economic realities. Accordingly, **the purpose and orientation of a "national urban policy" should be reconsidered. There are no "national urban problems," only an endless variety of local ones. Consequently, a centrally administered national urban policy that legitimizes activities inconsistent with the revitalization of the larger national economy may be ill advised.**

Priority should not be assigned to the implementation of a spatially sensitive policy effort designed to retard or reverse the emergence of new economic patterns and relationships within and among the nation's settlements. The federal government should assign greater priority to meeting the needs of the residents of the nation's communities rather than to reconciling or resolving the array of constituent intrametropolitan and interregional conflicts. The federal government should exercise its policy presence carefully so as not to exacerbate unnecessarily the circumstances facing certain localities and regions that cause them to lose population and economic vitality. **Where federal policies and programs are used to assist the transformation of local communities to achieve health and vitality at new population levels and with restructured economic bases, such national policies should endeavor to ameliorate the undesirable impacts of these transitions on people, primarily, and on places, secondarily.**

Although no national urban problems exist, myriad problems do exist within all localities and regions of the nation. Our nation's settlements, and the households, firms, and local governments within them, exhibit a bewildering diversity of conditions that reflect the confluence of long-term demographic, economic, and governance trends and that link them to emerging patterns of metropolitan and regional change. The forces underlying these transformations are relatively persistent and immutable. However, the local and regional problems left in their wake are not uniform in cause; therefore, the urban policies proposed as remedies cannot be expected to be uniform in consequence.

It is unlikely that the federal government can act wisely on behalf of the nation as a whole if economically healthy metropolitan areas are not appreciated because their vitality is discounted or obscured by a preoccupation with transforming core areas of central cities. Neither will the nation benefit if the newly prospering regions that historically have been economically depressed are defined as inimical to historically prosperous regions that are now experiencing relative economic decline. A national urban policy cannot be enunciated and implemented when the very national focus it should assume and the national well-being it should foster are sacrificed to a concern for the diverse fates and fortunes among cities, among metropolitan areas, among states, and among regions.

Certainly, there is merit in anticipating the locational consequences of federal government actions, but many federal policies aimed at promoting the efficiency and productivity of the nation have unavoidable negative consequences for certain localities and regions. Knowing that spatial tilts are embedded in federal policies provides no necessary justification for weeding them out. They often may be entirely justified. Indeed, anti-industry biases in federal policies may be more pernicious than anti-urban biases, given that the health of all places is directly or indirectly dependent on the strength of the larger economy. These tradeoffs should be clearly recognized, and choices should be made consistent with the functioning of the national system of settlements and the national economy, which benefits the entire country at the risk of abiding a series of smaller scale, and often painful, subnational adjustments. A national urban policy designed to place the swirl of local and regional concerns ahead of an overall concern for the nation is both inappropriate and ill advised.

Federal urban policy can be used to channel and target the enormous, if seldom adequate, resources of the federal government and to guide or influence the flows of private sector resources. Nonetheless, despite the importance of the government resources, and the far greater weight of the private resources that at times may be influenced, problems do not yield to massive infusions of resources alone. Rather, a great proportion of urban ills stems from inevitable competition for advantage among groups within localities and between regions. The litany of urban problems is a reflection of this underlying competition in a pluralistic urban society. The very competition that dictates our urban strengths may determine the nature of our urban ills, although not the character of the solutions to those ills. An explicit national urban policy can do little more than make that irony more salient.

The limits to what a federal urban policy effort can achieve are defined by several factors. First, **recognition should be made of the near immutability of the technological, economic, social, and demographic trends that herald the emergence of a postindustrial society and that are responsible for the transformation of our nation's settlements and life within them.** These major formative trends are likely to continue not only through the coming decade, but also well into the next century. Major deflection or reversal of these broad-gauge trends is not likely to result from purposive government action. **Clearly, on the basis of these trends, a federal policy of active anticipation, accommodation, and adjustment makes more sense than efforts to retard or reverse them. The efforts to revitalize those communities whose fortunes are adversely affected principally by the inadvertent consequences of past public policies are entirely justified, but these instances are judged to be rare. It is far more judicious to recognize that the major circumstances that characterize our nation's settlements have not been and will not be significantly dependent on what the federal government does or does not do.**

What should constitute a reasonable federal urban policy role in the light of domestic trends that are transforming this nation and transnational trends that are drawing us into closer community with the world? Policy responses to such complex and changing circumstances are inevitably difficult to conceive and develop. Not only do limits to what can be accomplished with policies and programs exist, but also in many substantive areas, the local readjustments may not require vigorous federal intervention. Accordingly, a proper federal presence in urban affairs should reflect a blend of actions to be avoided as well as actions to be taken. That powerful forces are creating multiple forms of distress in local communities and regions, and that they are not likely to be deflected or defused by public policy, do not inherently justify more or less federal urban policy. Rather, this situation serves as an argument for a different concept of what the federal urban policy role should be.

Redefining the Federal Role in Urban Policy

   The federal government can best assure the well-being of the nation's people and the vitality of the communities in which they live by striving to create and maintain a vibrant national economy characterized by an attractive investment climate that is conducive to high rates of economic productivity and growth and defined by low rates of inflation, unemployment, and dependency. Where disadvantage and inequality are selective and cumulative, federal efforts should be expended to ameliorate these consequences in ways that are consistent with developmental trends within the society and the economy as a whole.

   The federal government, in partnership with the business community and state and local governments, should carefully consider developing a policy perspective on industry in order to maintain a dynamic national economy and secure a strong role in the transforming international economy. The industrial bases of our nation's economic strength must be allowed to transform, and localities and regions should be assisted in anticipating and adjusting to national and international trends. A positive industry

101

policy should include national economic planning, a coherent science policy, and invigorated research and development efforts to nurture and enhance our existing comparative advantages within and between industrial sectors vis-a-vis other nations. Such efforts should acknowledge that much can be learned from certain individual firms that may be in the most challenged industrial sectors but are able to compete successfully in international and domestic markets. Increased productivity and employment growth, together with diminished inflation, will do more to benefit people in this nation, regardless of where they may live, than efforts to resist the local and regional impacts of a changing international economic order.

People-oriented national social policies that aim to aid people directly wherever they may live should be accorded priority over place-oriented national urban policies that attempt to aid people indirectly by aiding places directly. If the ultimate goal of federal policies and programs is to aid people in their adjustment to or migration from transforming local circumstances, the most direct and effective ways to do that should be chosen. **A national social policy should be based on key cornerstones, including a guaranteed job program for those who can work and a guaranteed cash assistance plan for both the "working poor" and those who cannot work.** Federal job creation, subsidies to private employers, and manpower training and retraining programs can significantly reduce minority, youth, and displaced worker unemployment. Where public employment programs are used, they should be considered a temporary supplement for and provide a transition into private sector employment. A federal guaranteed-income plan, implemented through either a negative income tax or a direct cash transfer program, would effectively and properly shift the welfare burden to the federal government, which can administer it more efficiently and with a greater capacity for responding to equity considerations than subnational governments.

Where the problems faced by people exist in such concentrations that the impacts of people-oriented social policies and programs are negated, or where communities bear the brunt of special circumstances (such as massive foreign immigration), federal funds should be carefully targeted to local governments and to the private sector to assist them in meeting collective needs. Nonetheless, the federal government should develop the will and capability to assist local governments in identifying both places that are unlikely to realize any significant improvement through targeted urban aid and appropriate strategies to disinvest public resources and to channel public and private resources to locations that retain the capacity to absorb and benefit from federal assistance.

These major social policy initiatives and realignments should largely substitute for, rather than add to, existing federal policies. Prime candidates among the federal urban (and rural) development assistance program efforts that should be scrutinized for eventual reduction or elimination are in the place-oriented policy domains, including economic development, community development and public facilities investment, housing, transportation, and development planning. Instrumentalities such as community development block grants, urban development action grants, general and countercyclical revenue sharing, CETA grants, and water and sewer construction grants can be useful tools for an adjustment process. However, their use can be justified only during localities' major transitions in size and function. In addition, such mechanisms should be tilted toward the goal of assisting localities to adjust to changing circumstances and should be used to supplement marginally, but not substitute for, efforts that aid people directly. Because guidelines for establishing timeframes for ending interim transitional efforts in view of a more spatially neutral federal presence will be exceedingly difficult to adopt, efforts should begin now.

It is important to realize that identifying tradeoffs among policies and programs with explicit urban foci is not sufficient. Tradeoffs among nominally nonurban federal policies and programs also should be considered, because they often have major, if inadvertent, urban impacts. Among the explicitly nonurban policies and programs that should be scrutinized for major restructuring or elimination are the panoply of in-kind benefits for the poor (such as legal aid services and Medicaid), the growing inventory of subsidies that indiscriminately aid the nonpoor as well as the poor (for example, veteran's benefits), protectionist measures for industry (trade barriers for manufacturers and price supports for farmers), and minimum wage legislation.

Although the original goals of each policy and program may be laudable in isolation, once set into place alongside all others, their aggregate result has been policy incoherence, inconsistency, internal contradictions, and inertia. Solutions regarded as permanent or sacrosanct tend to outlive and become poorly articulated with the characteristics of the problems that they were intended to address. The thrust of this extended proposal is that the problems of people and the places where they live can be handled in better ways than by continuing to tinker with hundreds of different programs that assist individuals, households, neighborhoods, businesses, and subnational governments. Although a "people-place" distinction may often be more apparent than real, the aim should be a reorientation of emphasis, which involves avoiding the temptation to use place-oriented assistance to prop up

103

localities rather than allowing them to transform. People are best assisted directly, and policies that best insulate people from or compensate them for painful transitional consequences should be emphasized.

Federal urban policy efforts should not necessarily be used to discourage the deconcentration and dispersal of industry and households from central urban locations. Interregional and intrametropolitan shifts of households and industry are essential to the efficient functioning of the national economic system on a scale that supercedes local and regional economies. Each emerging deconcentration trend is nothing more than an aggregate of countless choices by and actions of individuals, families, and firms influenced by social, cultural, and economic considerations; our public policy tools are least useful when attempting to alter in a predictable way what the individual household or firm will do. Yet, an inability to alter these developments should be appreciated apart from the fact that their net impact is probably positive and beneficial. The ongoing deconcentration processes that leave very undesirable local consequences in their wake justify a federal policy role that principally attends to these consequences, rather than flails against the change processes that generate them.

The relocation of population and economic vitality to nonmetropolitan and previously rural areas also should not be discouraged. The current revitalization of traditionally rural areas should neither obscure the fact that much of the traditional basis for urban-rural distinctions no longer exists, nor veil the fact that much of formerly rural America remains unaffected by expanding and diversified economic bases. Although the poor of this nation are largely city-bound, the incidence of poverty in rural areas still exceeds that in urban areas.

The energy and environmental implications of the continuing trends toward relatively low-density development in new growth areas and the thinning out of existing high-density areas do not unequivocally justify the need for a national effort to encourage reconcentration in historically central locations. The emergence of decentralized social and economic systems, which encompass increasing scope and territory and dictate that new, more specialized functions be performed by cities, should generally be encouraged. Although energy and environmental considerations will and should assert themselves in important policy debates in the coming decade and beyond, as yet little compelling and unambiguous empirical evidence exists to justify explicit public policy designed to alter the way in which our nation's communities grow and contract. Conservation of existing energy and environmental resources is not necessarily inconsistent with, and may even be enhanced by, the shift to lower density development, small-scale reconcentration in new growth areas, and the thinning out of large-scale, centrally located concentrations of people and activities. Nonetheless, the federal government should not abdicate its responsibility to assist localities and states in anticipating and countering the negative consequences that low-density development may have in some locations, including those instances where prime agricultural land is invaded indiscriminately by urban uses.

Federal policies should not be revamped, without careful consideration given to their primary functions and net effects, simply because unintended or inadvertent "anti-urban" consequences are discovered. Bending federal policies that do not have an explicit urban focus to serve locational or spatial outcomes may be undesirable. Although countless federal policies initiate a barrage of unintended anti-urban effects, these policy thrusts most often have simply reinforced larger demographic and economic trends or marginally increased the pace with which they have unfolded.

In the end, the federal government does not have that much control over what happens to localities and regions. There is little justification for using explicit urban policies to do more than assist people primarily and places secondarily to anticipate and adjust to the emergence of a continually transforming national economy and society. Federal policies, including investment tax credits and environmental regulations, have important narrow sectoral goals that may be unwisely sacrificed if they are manipulated to secure specific urban outcomes.

In close partnership with the private sector, the federal government should develop strategies to assist localities in adjusting to economic-base transformation and population change. In a federal policy lexicon, "development policy" should be expanded to imply policy-guided local contraction and not simply local revitalization and expansion. Policy-guided contraction and disinvestment can help to ease the impact of decline on individuals and local institutions and to position communities for regaining their health at new lower levels of population and industrial activity.

The federal government should acknowledge that the problems of population and economic growth can be as troublesome and painful as those of shrinkage. Shifts in population and economic activity, which current policy instrumentalities probably cannot reverse, pose specific adjustment problems for metropolitan and nonmetropolitan communities in all regions. Both growth and decline present opportunities to local governments to become better articulated with their populations and economic bases through carefully planned expansion or contraction. **The federal government should assist communities during**

their transition and adjustment to new levels of population and economic activity.

Federal policies aimed at achieving beneficial urban outcomes should be consistent with efforts to ensure a strong national economy and to implement national programs in health, welfare, housing, transportation, energy, environmental protection, and local governmental assistance that are consistent with dominant trends. These policy domains should not use allocational strategies for federal efforts that attempt to counter larger social and economic transformations or to maintain specific local or regional advantages that are slowly being eroded in the course of metropolitan and regional development. Nonetheless, the federal government should be fully sensitive to the fact that even though certain large-scale transformations bode well for the nation, they do imply serious transitional distress for some localities.

Accordingly, **the federal government should continue to assist localities in providing basic services to local residents.** Meeting the collective needs of citizens wherever they live will continue to require close federal-local cooperation. **The federal government should refrain wherever possible from assigning new responsibilities to localities unless they also provide the resources that localities need to meet those obligations.** This intergovernmental relationship recognizes both the well developed capacity of the federal tax system to collect and disperse revenues efficiently and the developing capacity of localities to provide the necessary services in the most efficient manner. Although much place-oriented federal assistance to localities is ill advised to the extent that it is expended to reverse the largely inevitable shrinkage of larger and older communities, some short-term federal transitional assistance to localities is justified to assist them in meeting the expanding range of their responsibilities. As localities experience difficulty in funding basic services or in meeting the financial obligations incurred through federal orders and mandates, the principle of federal adjustment assistance to localities should be inviolate.

Improved access to jobs involves helping people relocate to take advantage of economic opportunities in other places, as well as retraining them to take advantage of economic opportunity in their own communities. Enhancing the mobility of Americans to enable them to relocate to areas where economic opportunity exists should receive greater attention. Accordingly, **a people-to-jobs strategy should be crafted with priority over, but in concert with, the jobs-to-people strategy that serves as a major theme in current federal urban policy.** Greater emphasis on developing a policy of assisted migration would help under-employed and displaced workers who wish to migrate to

106

locations of long-term economic growth. This option is especially necessary for residents of severely distressed, older industrial cities facing relatively permanent contraction of their economic and population bases.

States should be encouraged and aided in their efforts to assist local governments, as well as their individual and corporate residents, to adjust to changing social and economic circumstances. The nation's cities are national assets that will continue to perform vital, although changing, functions for the United States. Although transforming socially and economically, cities remain the legal creations of the states. In past decades, many subnational governments have improved substantially their capacities to implement economic, community, and manpower development policies. Intergovernmental relationships in the coming decade should preserve the spirit of the federal-local government ties without undermining the emergence of state governments as key urban policy partners.

The State Government Role

Localities should be encouraged to reexamine their municipal service packages and their funding and delivery arrangements. Much local fiscal distress can be traced to an inability to adjust public service infrastructures to changing population size and composition. Municipal service arrangements should either expand in growing communities or contract in shrinking communities in ways that give localities the flexibility to adjust to future changes. Growing localities should be encouraged to consider carefully the breadth of functions and depth of responsibilities that they wish to assume, thereby avoiding a ritualistic imitation of those local governments that assumed their responsibilities in an earlier historical era. Greater reliance on private sector delivery of public services and the transfer of fiscal/administrative responsibility for selected functions to other levels of government should be carefully considered.

The Local Government Role

The patterns of relationships between localities, counties, states, and the federal government have grown increasingly complex. Responsibilities for funding and administration have become hopelessly intergovernmentalized. The unfortunate and inescapable consequence of our broader, bigger, and deeper federal aid system is intergovernmental overload. This report endorses the general recommendations made by the Advisory Commission on Intergovernmental Relations aimed at the decongestion of the federal system.[2]

Implementing Federal Urban Policy: Partners and Partnerships

The federal role in urban policy should allow for the sorting out of roles and responsibilities among levels of government and between the public and private sectors. Once those reassignments are made, policy and program activity should seek to abide by and to maintain those assignments. In addition to seeking to reintroduce distinctions between federal and subnational responsibilities, efforts should proceed to decide under what conditions and to what extent state and local budgets should become dependent on federal revenues.

Any policies targeted at the nation's communities should engage the federal government as a policy partner with other levels of government and with the private sector to assist people (primarily), places, business, and political jurisdictions (secondarily) to cope with changing circumstances. The resulting policy division of labor should continue to emphasize the decentralization of federal power and the assignment to each partner of the tasks that it can best undertake.

The federal level of government is relatively efficient at enunciating broad policy goals and raising revenues for distribution to subnational levels of government which, in turn, can best define specific program features. Over time many subnational governments have expanded their capacities to initiate and to implement localized community and economic development efforts without complex federal controls. Local general purpose governments should continue to be the principal policy implementers at the local level, and policy instruments that encourage local initiative consistent with national purpose should be emphasized. Despite problems associated with granting wider discretion to local governments, on balance accepting local judgments is wiser than implementing federal policies that are relatively unable to be articulated with local circumstances.

The federal government should retain responsibility for ensuring that local initiatives, while reflecting local circumstances, are consistent with national goals—particularly in the area of civil rights. The nation needs to develop ways of accomplishing this valid purpose without requiring duplication of the federal government's organizational complexity at the local level. The public sector should endeavor to enhance and encourage private sector vitality and, where necessary, to alleviate its undesirable consequences without hampering that vitality.

Although place-oriented federal urban and rural development policies and programs eventually should be reduced in significance in favor of more people-oriented national economic and social policies, during the transition between emphases, the former should become more coordinated and coherent, with greater emphasis on policy consistency than on level of program funding. While housing, transportation, and urban economic, community, and manpower development programs marshal relatively meager resources in efforts to ameliorate the impacts of unfolding demographic and economic trends, their potency can be enhanced through better organization and consolidation. General fiscal and monetary policies, transfer payments to individuals, and development assistance to the public and private sectors have their collective impact diluted by indefinite lines of responsibility, divergent delivery systems, and program procedures (including idiosyncratic funding cycles, planning requirements, and eligibility criteria) that often differ and even conflict. Consequently, the efforts of subnational governments and the decisions of private sector actors are unnecessarily hampered by gaps, overlaps, and shifting goals at the federal level.

1. R.B. Miller, "The Federal Role in Cities: The New Deal Years," *Commentary,* Washington, D.C.: National Council for Urban Economic Development (July 1979):110.
2. Advisory Commission on Intergovernmental Relations, *An Agenda for American Federalism: Restoring Confidence and Competence.* (Washington, D.C.: U.S. Government Printing Office, forthcoming).

Biographies

Robert S. Benson is President of Children's World, Inc., which owns and operates child care centers in 95 locations nationally. Mr. Benson received his B.A. from Harvard College and his M.B.A. degree from the Harvard Business School. Previously, he has worked for the Office of the Secretary of Defense and has been a community organizer for the National Urban Coalition, where he created the National Priorities Project that produced the report, *Counterbudget: A Blueprint for Changing National Priorities.* Mr. Benson has served on the committees and boards of several organizations concerned with early childhood development.

Robert S. Benson

Charles E. Bishop is President of the University of Houston System. Dr. Bishop is a graduate of Berea College in agricultural education, has earned a Masters degree in agricultural economics from the University of Kentucky, and received his Ph.D. in economics from the University of Chicago. Previously, he has served as President of the University of Arkansas System, Chancellor at the University of Maryland and Vice President for Research and Public Service in the University of North Carolina System. Dr. Bishop has worked on numerous national and regional task forces on agricultural, labor, and rural issues, including the National Advisory Commission on Rural Poverty and the White House Conference on Balanced National Growth and Economic Development.

Charles E. Bishop

Pastora San Juan Cafferty is a Professor at the School of Social Service Administration at the University of Chicago, where she has created and directed a graduate program in urban policy since 1974. Ms. Cafferty also serves on the Committee on Public Policy Studies at the university. Ms. Cafferty has served in the offices of the Secretary of the U.S. Department of Transportation and of Housing and Urban Development, as well as on the Board of Directors of the Chicago Urban Transit District. She has consulted and written numerous articles in the fields of bilingualism and education and has done extensive work on the subject of Hispanics in America.

Pastora San Juan Cafferty

111

Ruth J. Hinerfeld is President of the League of Women Voters. Before her election as president in 1978, Ms. Hinerfeld served as the League's first Vice President of Legislative Activities, as Chairperson of the League's International Relations Committee, and as the League's United Nations Observer. Ms. Hinerfeld is a graduate of Vassar College and the Harvard-Radcliffe Program in Business Administration. She was appointed by Presidents Gerald R. Ford and Jimmy Carter to serve on the White House Advisory Committee for Trade Negotiations. In addition, Ms. Hinerfeld has served as Secretary of the United Nations Association of the United States of America and as a member of the U.S. delegation to the World Conference on the U.N. Decade for Women. She is also a member of the Overseas Development Council, Leadership Conference on Civil Rights, and the National Petroleum Council.

Ruth J. Hinerfeld

Frank Pace, Jr., is President and Chief Executive Officer of the International Executive Service Corps and also Chairman and Chief Executive Officer of the National Executive Service Corps. Mr. Pace is a graduate of Princeton University and received his LL.B. from the Harvard University Law School. Previously, he was the Director of the U.S. Bureau of the Budget, the Secretary of the Army under President Harry S. Truman, the President and Chairman of the Board of General Dynamics Corporation, and a past Chairman of the Board of the Corporation for Public Broadcasting. Mr. Pace served as Vice Chairman of the President's Commission on National Goals, formed by President Dwight D. Eisenhower to outline national objectives for the 1960s.

Frank Pace, Jr.

Donald A. Hicks is Senior Professional Staff for the Panel on Policies and Prospects for Metropolitan and Non-metropolitan America in the Eighties. Dr. Hicks received his B.A. from Indiana University and his Ph.D. in sociology from the University of North Carolina-Chapel Hill. He is currently on leave from the University of Texas-Dallas, where he is an Associate Professor of sociology and political economy, and he has worked in the Office of the Governor of North Carolina. Dr. Hicks has published numerous articles in a variety of policy science and urban issue areas, including problems in metropolitan service delivery, suburban "exploitation" of central cities, patterns of residential relocation, and public-private sector alliances in municipal service delivery. In addition, his research interests include issues in quasi-experimental research design and policy impact analysis.

Donald A. Hicks

112

Index